THE LUSCIOUS LOW-FAT COOKBOOK

THE LUSCIOUS LOW-FAT COOKBOOK

ALISON ROSE AND TONY GUY

Vermilion
LONDON

This book is dedicated to all those people who've wanted access to easy to understand low-fat recipes and low-fat lifestyle information and could never get it. This book is for you.

3 5 7 9 10 8 6 4 2

First published in 2002 by Vermilion, an imprint of Ebury Press, Random House, 20 Vauxhall Bridge Road, London SW1V 2SA www.randomhouse.co.uk

Random House Australia (Pty) Limited 20 Alfred Street, Milsons Point, Sydney, New South Wales 2061, Australia

Random House New Zealand Limited 18 Poland Road, Glenfield, Auckland 10, New Zealand

Random House South Africa (Pty) Limited Endulini, 5a Jubilee Road, Parktown 2193, South Africa

The Random House Group Limited Reg. No. 954009

Papers used by Vermilion are natural, recyclable products made from wood grown in sustainable forests.

Printed and bound in Portugal by Printer Portuguesa

A CIP catalogue record for this book is available from the British Library.

ISBN 0 09 188283 4

The information provided in this book is meant as a guide only.

People embarking on a diet should consult their doctor before they start.

The nutritional analysis provided in this book is based on average servings.

The fat content may vary dependent on portion size or products used.

In producing our nutritional analysis we have used average nutritional breakdowns.

CONTENTS

WHAT IS A HEALTHY LOW-FAT DIET?

This is a great question. Most people think they eat healthily but are daily doing battle with hidden food problems ... too much salt, not enough fibre, too much fat and a confusion about what food they can eat and how much of it they should eat. When they know this they feel overwhelmed about how to achieve it all as well as feed the kids, get the train, do their job, do the shopping, meet with colleagues, make that deadline, sleep ... and check their e-mail. So here it is: the quick and easy low-fat diet. Let's start by looking at a healthy diet. The best way to understand this is to recognise that there are five food groups:

❶ Fruit and vegetables ❷ Breads and cereals

❸ Dairy products ❹ Protein ❺ Fats and oils

To be healthy we need to eat some of each of these each day. To help understand how much of each food group you should eat, use the inverted pyramid system:

Fruit and vegetables: 5 servings or more a day.

Breads and cereals, rice and pasta include some with each meal.

Milk and dairy products: 2-3 servings a day.

Meat or Protein: 2-3 servings a day.

Fats and oils: small amounts only.

What's a serving?

This is a question everyone asks. Healthy eaters around the world say they eat so many servings of this or that, but is a serving half an apple, three apples or a whole box full? Well, we were confused, so here is a great serving guide.

Fruit and vegetables

One serving equals:
- ◆ 2 handfuls leafy salad
- ◆ ½ cup raw or cooked vegetables, e.g. 1 carrot, 1 courgette, 10 cm cucumber

- ◆ 1 whole piece of fruit
- ◆ half the juice of a freshly squeezed orange
- ◆ 50 g canned fruit
- ◆ 25 g dried fruit

So have 1 mixed juice a day, an apple, and a 100-g bag of dried apricots and you are done.

Breads and cereals, rice and pasta

One serving equals:

- ◆ 50 g cooked cereal
- ◆ 50 g pasta
- ◆ 50 g cooked rice
- ◆ 1 slice wholemeal bread
- ◆ Half a large bread roll or one small bread roll
- ◆ 1 small jacket potato

So a slice of toast at breakfast, a pasta salad at lunch, and some rice at dinner and you are done.

Milk, yoghurt and cheese

One serving equals:

- ◆ 150 ml yoghurt
- ◆ 200 ml milk
- ◆ 25 g cheese

So a carton of yoghurt mid-morning, a latte to get you going and a cube of low-fat cheese will just do it.

Protein

One serving equals:

- ◆ 200 g baked beans
- ◆ 2 eggs or a 5 egg white omelette (see page 34)
- ◆ 100 g tuna or salmon in brine
- ◆ 75 g lean ham, chicken or turkey (1 to 2 slices)
- ◆ 40 g of low-fat cheese
- ◆ 100 g soya protein replacement

A Typical Day's Diet

A typical day's low-fat diet can seem a bit daunting, so here is an example of a typical day, which, you can see, gives you plenty of protein and other nutrients. During the day drink lots of water. If you find water boring, try flavouring it with no-sugar juice. Hot water and lemon is a great kick starter for the day

BREAKFAST
Mixed fruit juice
Cereal
Toast
Piece of fruit

MID-MORNING SNACK
Low-fat yoghurt with banana
Low-fat cino or latte

LUNCH
200 g wholemeal pasta with low-fat lemon mayo and lean chicken mixed through
Mixed fruit juice
Side salad of tomato, lettuce and olives in brine with three small cubes of feta cheese

MID-AFTERNOON
100 g bag of dried mixed fruit or sultanas or small bag of sunflower and pumpkin seeds and small pot low-fat yoghurt

DINNER
Lean turkey and vegetable stir-fry with wild honeyed rice
Peaches filled with strawberry fromage frais

AFTER DINNER
Low-fat hot choc

Fat-finding mission

It may seem like a mission impossible cutting through all the fat to get to the heart of the matter, but before you start living your low-fat lifestyle you need to be able to differentiate the good fats from the bad fats.

The fact of the matter is that a little bit of fat is good for you. It is an important part of your daily diet. This fat provides us with fat-soluble vitamins like A, D and E and essential fats, which the human body just can't make.

The problem is that we eat too much fat. Obesity levels are skyrocketing in the United Kingdom and other Western nations, and so is the incidence of heart disease and other health problems linked to being overweight.

So what is a good fat?

Good fats come in two forms – polyunsaturated and monounsaturated. These are important for a balanced diet.

Polyunsaturates

Polyunsaturates are good fats which provide us with essential fatty acids. For example, fatty acids in vegetable oils can help your body fight high blood cholesterol. These types of fats are found in:

1 **Oil rich fish** like salmon, sardines and mackerel.
2 **Vegetable oils** like sunflower, soya oil and corn oil, as well as spreads made from things like nuts contain polyunsaturates

Top tips for eating polyunsaturates

1 **Don't overdo it.** Polyunsaturates are still a fat so eat only small amounts.
2 **Butter replacement spreads** that contain vegetable oils are a good way to get your daily dose of polyunsaturates.
3 **Eat some oily fish** once a week and remember it doesn't matter if it is fresh, smoked or canned.
4 **Remember,** tuna in oil in a can doesn't count as an oily fish.

Monounsaturates

Most researchers will tell you that monounsaturated fats are not vital to your diet, but the key here is that are a great replacement for the bad fat – saturated fat. You can find monounsaturated fat in:

1 Rapeseed oil.
2 Olive oil.
3 Nuts and seeds.

Top tips for eating monounsaturates
1 **Again,** don't overdo it
2 **Think** of your monounsaturated fats as your bad fat replacer
3 **Olive oil** in small quantities is good for cooking, so use this rather than butter in the frying pan

Bad fats

Saturated fats

As the appointed fat police this is the fat we want locked away. We don't need this fat and eating too much of it has been linked to heart disease. It is also the 'spare tire' culprit. You find saturated fats in:
1 **Cream,** full fat milk, hard cheeses and cream-filled yoghurt
2 **Lard,** dripping, butter and even margarine
3 **Rich cream cakes** and biscuits – especially chocolate ones
4 **Some savoury snacks** and nuts
5 **Fatty cuts** of meat

Luscious advice

- **Always check the label** – the fat section should be separated into saturated and unsaturated. If the food is low-fat but has a very high saturated fat level keep away from it. This is what we call a hidden fat.

- **Try to eat less** than 10% of your fat intake as a saturated fat and **cut all the fat off meat.**

- **At restaurants** ask the chef what type of 'oil' they use in their kitchens – you are entitled to know. After all, a tomato pasta is great, but if the chef has fried the tomatoes in butter then what is the point?

Setting your fat quota

Many people are consuming 40-50 per cent of their daily food intake as fat (which could be as much as 165 g per day – over a week, the equivalent of three tubs of margarine). But many health experts recommend that our fat intake should be no more than 30 per cent of our total daily consumption. If you wish to lose weight, it needs to be lower – around 20 per cent. Some experts say that for best weight loss results, daily fat intake can be as low as 15 or even 10 per cent. However, if you wish to go on an extremely low-fat diet, you should consult a dietitian or your doctor first.

To determine the best intake of fat for you, we have set a fat quota – we call it our Luscious Limit. Your Luscious Limit can be designed to:

- **Lose weight:** A Luscious Limiter.
- **Maintain weight:** A Luscious Life Limit.
- **Gain weight:** yep, some people have to and they get to try the Luscious Limitless quota.

Decide on one of these three and you can calculate how many grams of fat you should restrict yourself to each day. The average recommended fat intake for weight maintenance or a Luscious Life Limit is 63g for women and 83g for men (see also the chart, below). Remember, we all need some fat in our diet so the body can function properly, and this fat should naturally be the good fat we talk about in this book.

Maximum daily fat intake at a glance

	Small build		Medium build		Large build	
	Women	Men	Women	Men	Women	Men
To lose weight be a **Luscious Limiter** (20% of total energy intake)	38 g	51 g	41 g	57 g	47 g	72 g
To maintain weight go for the **Luscious Life Limit** (30% of total energy intake)	56 g	76 g	61 g	85 g	67 g	90 g

To calculate your daily fat intake, you need to know how much fat is in each item of food you eat. This all adds up to your daily 'fat quota', which varies depending on your age, sex, weight, and whether you want to lose weight or simply maintain the weight you are now. To qualify as low-fat, the fat content of a food should be 5 per cent or less – in other words, 5 g or less per 100 g. Most food labels now contain this information, and you should always check until you become familiar with which foods contain 'hidden fats'. However, if food isn't labelled, it's difficult to know just how fatty it is. To help you, we've compiled a list of some common foods and their fat contents. These are to be found in the Luscious Lists on page 154.

Whenever you shop, stop and read the label. It's important to check the fat content per 100 g and per pack. Try different brands because often there are discrepancies. If there is no nutritional information then complain or ring the manufacturer – they should provide you with it. Often we can help, so e-mail info@luscious.co.uk if you really get stuck.

Get motivated – you know you can do it

Eating low-fat for Tony and me became a way of life not through religious zeal but simply because of a desire to eat more healthily. I mean, how many times have you come away from a meal at a restaurant feeling:

- **Bloated?**
- **The meal** was full of fat?
- **No care** was taken in preparation?
- **You got** a small serving?
- **It was** full of nasties?

How many times have you searched the high street for lunch thinking:

- **Why can't** I get a nice low-fat sandwich?
- **Why do** the fried foods smell so gross?
- **I wish** fast-fried food wasn't so accessible?
- **Why is** it so hard to make a good salad?

This is why we set up Luscious. But eating low-fat does take motivation. Motivation to:

- **Do** the shopping.
- **Prepare** a meal list.
- **Check** the fat contents.
- **Not** be lured to easy high-fat options.

The key is to make eating low-fat as easy as possible. That means motivation. So to help you, here are ten top reasons to eat low-fat food:

1 **You'll feel** healthier.
2 **You'll get** better cuts of meat.
3 **You'll learn** more about your body.
4 **You'll have** more energy.
5 **You'll ensure** you get a balanced diet.
6 **You'll be** less susceptible to heart disease and other problems linked to being overweight.
7 **You'll detox** your body of nasties.
8 **You'll achieve** a personal goal.
9 **You'll make** a real difference in your life by knowing you have confidently taken control of a problem or concern and found a viable and enjoyable solution.
10 **You'll lose** weight.

Why do it?

Because you can and your body deserves it.
You'll get curves in the right places and be able to buy that outfit.
A lean bloke or great looking woman is likely to get more looks from potential partners.
You get to show off in the gym, on the beach, etc. etc.

Stay motivated – it's tough

The key to staying motivated is to get a low-fat buddy. Find someone to join you on your low-fat lifestyle change and then you can:

• **Plan** menus together.
• **Praise** each other on small achievements.
• **Punish** those who fail fridge checks with 50 extra sit-ups.
• **Work** out together.
• **Conduct** spot checks on each others fridges.

Make a list of the low-fat goals you would like to achieve and every time you reach one, reward yourself – not with fatty foods but with a movie, a new outfit, a book, a walk in the park, a meditation class. To get started, here are the first week's goals we set ourselves (see opposite). Use this same list or create your own.

Tick off each goal as you achieve it and once the week's list is complete congratulate yourself and be proud … you know, we don't do that enough. Then it's time to start again. Your list of goals will probably change from week to week, but keep on going – we promise you, IT'S WORTH IT.

Alison and Tony's low-fat goals

Goal	Tick when done
Check cupboards and **get rid of high-fat food**	
Check fridge and **get rid of high-fat food**	
Stock cupboards with **low-fat basics**	
Stock fridge with **low-fat basics**	
Understand and work out how to ensure you get the right servings in each food group (see page 6)	
Make **a low-fat menu list** for a day	
Make **a low-fat weekly menu**	
Choose and mark **your favourite low-fat recipes** in this book	
Make a list of **your high-fat weaknesses**	
Join **a gym**	
Find a **low-fat buddy**	

High energy and how to get it on a low-fat lifestyle

- **Do you** often lose concentration?
- **Do you** think you don't get enough sleep each night?
- **Are you** rarely ready to go and wide awake within 20 minutes of waking up?
- **Do you need** something to get you going in the morning?
- **Do you need** chocolate, sugar, tea or coffee to keep you going through the day?
- **Do you get** irritable if you haven't eaten?
- **Do you avoid** exercise because you don't have enough energy?
- **Are you** tired all the time?

If you answered yes to four or more of these questions, then you need to **boost** your energy levels. But first you need to understand why they are getting depleted. When you get stressed or work hard you are using energy. That means your energy stores get depleted. Think about how you feel when you eat chocolate; you get a quick high and feel like you have a great deal of energy, followed by another low. This high and low is bad for your system, and if you don't replace your energy stores you'll continue feeling tired. Chocolate and caffeine fixes just won't do it. You need to look at an eating pattern that provides your body with clean energy in a continuous fashion. The best way to do that is through low-fat healthy eating.

This means you need to ensure you get your optimal intake of nutrients and vitamins and that you take in slow-releasing carbohydrates. You should also avoid stimulants and things that depress your system. Fried fatty food does that. So that means changing your eating habits.

Low-fat lifestyle journal

We both recommend a lifestyle journal. We know this is not Bridget Jones but she was our inspiration. If you log on to www.luscious.co.uk you can download the journal that we keep on it. It will help you keep track of your fat intake, your favourite recipes, the best restaurants and perhaps your personal business as well.

Myths and mysteries

'Now I can't go out to dinner.'
This is wrong, wrong, wrong. You must eat dinner but you need to think small. This means small portions and check out our rights and wrongs on eating out. Let them guide you.

'Carbohydrates are out.'
Your body needs carbohydrates, like it needs fats, water, minerals and protein. It is all about moderation.

'I have to give up the booze.'
This is rubbish. A couple of glasses a week won't do you any harm. In fact, in some countries like France, red wine is seen as medicinal. Alcohol is fat-free but the sugar in it means calories, so again think moderation.

'What if I binge? All the good work is gone.'
This is also wrong. You need to think carefully about why you are falling off the low-fat wagon. Perhaps you need to deal with the binges. Keeping a food journal helps (see opposite). It gives you an idea of what you eat – and remember we all like a treat every now and then … it boosts moral and it can be a reward.

'I can't eat after dark.'
Some dieticians say that your body slows down after dark. Don't eat a big meal before you go to sleep but understand your eating patterns.

'Sugar is out.'
Some diets say you have to cut all sugar, some suggest using sugar replacements. We say cut out as much sugar as possible.

'Fast food is out.'
We don't recommend you eat fast food all the time but remember that salads can have more fat in them than a cheeseburger because of high-fat salad dressings. Ask your favourite fast-food provider for their lowest-fat products.

'I have to count calories and weigh things.'
A low-fat lifestyle is just that – a lifestyle. This book aims to help you learn about adopting this lifestyle so you can live it and not worry about calorie counting.

LOW-FAT LIVING

The thing about a low-fat lifestyle is that we suggest you eat more but in small amounts. It's called constructive grazing. Also understand what causes your snack attack. It could be a food sensitivity, hyperglycemia or simply boredom. See the box on snack attacks and how to start dealing with them (opposite)

Living a low-fat lifestyle is also all about conquering your fear. Fear the food will taste like cardboard? Fear it will be too hard in this stress-filled world? Fear you'll deprive yourself or others of yummy food? The key is learn some luscious life tips – rules you can use on a daily basis that make living low-fat that much easier.

Easy-to-use low-fat rules

Learn to drink non-fat milk

Those people who have said that low-fat milk or skimmed milk tastes awful, can't make a cappuccino or will make a latte taste bad don't know what they are talking about. A frothy skimmed milk cino is fantastic yet many cafés don't stock it because you require a little more skill in frothing the milk. But just think, if we demand it, people will have to provide it. Non-fat milk is key to a low-fat diet – it's a great fat replacement, and is good on cereal and in tea and coffee. A skinny hot choc with extra froth is still decadent but without the cream ... the froth does the same thing. Take 250 ml of skimmed milk and heat it in a pan. As the milk heats add 1 teaspoon low-fat chocolate sprinkles or low-fat chocolate sauce topping. When just about boiling pour into a blender and whizz until fluffy. To enhance that taste sensation, add some mint or orange.

Use low-fat mayonnaise

Low-fat mayonnaise has 1 g of fat per tablespoon. It is fine on sandwiches and mixed with strong-tasting foods like tuna. Mix equal parts low-fat mayonnaise with drained non-fat or low-fat yogurt. This really cuts the fat content of the mayonnaise and makes an excellent substitute for high-fat mayonnaise in potato salad and other mayonnaise-based salads.

Salad dressings

Most people think if they order a salad rather than a main meal at dinner they are eating low-fat. Wrong. The problem is that most salads come with high-fat

What encourages you to indulge in a snack attack?

1 **Boredom?**
2 **Anger?**
3 **Stress?**
4 **Pressure at work?**
5 **Bad news?**
6 **Relationship problems?**
7 **Bingeing?**
8 **Bad body image?**
9 **Self-hatred?**

Ways to deal with the problems

- **We often eat when we are not hungry** because of the reasons above. The most important thing is to replace high-fat snacks with low-fat options. Fruit is the easiest alternative – fresh or dried – or try any of the low-fat snacks given throughout this book.

- **Exercise is also important.** Running to the store for a chocolate works better if you run past it, down the road and into the gym.

- **You should also consider getting an exercise buddy** and a fridge buddy. You can exercise together and provide mutual support – and you can check each's other fridges.

dressings and that throws your low-fat lifestyle right out the window. In fact, a caesar salad with fried croutons and a creamy high-fat dressing can contain up to 50 g of fat. The key is to ask for the dressing on the side and for it to be a low-fat option. In this book, you'll find some fantastic low-fat dressing recipes, and there are some wonderful dressings available ready-made in shops

Balsamic vinegar

Balsamic vinegar is a great salad dressing all by itself. It is also great sprinkled on ripe tomatoes with shreds of basil on top. To add flavour to balsamic vinegar buy in bulk quantity from a health store and transfer to smaller bottles together with any of the following ingredients:

- **thyme**
- **rosemary**
- **chilli**
- **nuts** – whatever you like.

These bottles also make fabulous low-fat gifts.

Sour cream
If you eat a dish where sour cream is an important taste ingredient or you need it for cooking, use low-fat sour cream or mix sour cream with low-fat yoghurt.

Yoghurt
Non-fat yoghurt can become an essential ingredient in a low-fat lifestyle. It can be added to creams, is a wonderful topping for jacket potatoes and tacos, and I often use it when making a quiche instead of all the cream. Don't forget, it makes a great fat replacment in cakes. Low-fat yoghurt mixed with honey is also a yummy sweet treat. Create sour cream or yoghurt flavour combos by mixing in chilli or other herbs to add zest to your low-fat meal.

Low-fat cheese
Hunt for low-fat cheese in the supermarket. You'll discover that most of the low-fat cheeses (anywhere from 2.5-5 g of fat per 100 g) are an acceptable substitute for their high-fat counterparts. They work well in cooking and they melt well. Vegan cheese is often lower in fat and good vegan cheeses taste great.

Eggs
One egg contains 5 g of fat but remember that the fat in the egg is in the yolk. You can replace the yolk in cooking by combining more egg white with a whole egg. Try making egg white omelettes (see page 34) – they are fun to eat, have almost no fat and are very Hollywood, baby.

The wonder that is the mini-meal
Mini-meals are vital in a low-fat lifestyle. We advocate eating five to six mini-meals a day rather than three large ones. Mini-meals help beat the boredom barrier and keep energy levels level. They also protect you against crushing lethargy after a

large meal and against sugar lows, which rob you of enthusiasm and which many people suffer from. With mini-meals you will also burn about 10 per cent more calories a day. This is due to the thermal effect of feeding, which burns off calories as heat. So go for smaller meals more often. Research has also suggested that it is actually healthier to eat mini-meals because:

- **Mini-meals** stabilise your blood sugars.
- **They put** less pressure on your heart.
- **They put** less pressure on your digestive system.
- **They also** help to diminish cravings.

Think of a mini-meal as an entrée-sized portion. Six entrées a day is better than three big meals. When people are trying to lose weight, often they eat a meal at night and feel guilty because they feel bloated and fat. Mini-meals do not bloat your stomach and so help combat bad self-image and its demoralising effect. Throughout this book there are a great many low-fat snacks – just flick through the pages and take your pick.

The kitchen cupboard conundrum

The key to low-fat cooking is having what you need on hand. What that means is ensuring you have the right spices, sauces and raw ingredients for easy, no-fuss, low-fat cooking. Now, I hear a few groans because we are all busy and most of us hate going to the supermarket as you always have to queue and then get everything home afterwards. So what we suggest is that you do one big shop and get the kitchen cupboard stocked … and then value-add with fresh ingredients when you need them.

At the back of the book (see page 152) we have prepared a list of essential ingredients. You can copy down this list or print it directly from our website. At the bottom of the list is a section for your fresh ingredients. Whatever recipes you choose, check them first and write in what fresh ingredients you need – it makes planning much easier.

What's my option?

'What's my option?' is a bit like a TV game show. In this case, the prize is a yummy low-fat meal and the key is guessing the low-fat replacement for your high-fat favourite.

High-fat food	Low-fat replacement
Oil	Oil and water mix. Same goes for butter if you have to sauté
Cream	Vanilla yoghurt; skimmed, evaporated milk whisked till light and fluffy; low-fat crème fraiche
Sour cream	Low-fat sour cream; low-fat plain yoghurt
Coconut milk	Low-fat coconut milk or half coconut milk mixed with skimmed milk, or in extreme cases skimmed milk soaked overnight in coconut and then drained
Coconut	Use coconut flavouring or soak coconut in water or skimmed milk overnight and drain
Chocolate bar	Sultanas; dried fruit; dried tropical fruit; yoghurt-covered craving raisins; yoghurt-covered apricots; reduced-fat chocolate bars
Muesli	Make your own at home to ensure no added oils; dried fruit is great for this
Double cream with a desert	Low-fat custard
Milk	Use half-fat or non-fat option
Latte	Ask for skimmed milk at a restaurant
Hot choc	Ask for skimmed milk at a restaurant
Cappuccino	Ask for skimmed milk at a restaurant
Cream cheese	Low-fat cream cheese
Mayonnaise	Low-fat mayo mixed with herbs to add flavour; low-fat Greek yoghurt mixed with herbs
Meat marinades	Oil and water flavour combos given on page 27
Salad dressing	Low-fat options (see page 17); balsamic vinegar (see page 18)
Oils and butter	Apple purée, prune purée or mixture of half apple purée; for cakes half low-fat margarine
Cakes	Feel the urge? Then try the biscuits and cakes given on pages 16 onwards
High fat muffins	Luscious low-fat muffins (see page 118)
Doughnut	Bagel with jam; crumpet with banana and honey mash

Biscuits	Reach for dried fruit, low-fat yoghurt or low-fat biscuits (see page 122)
Chocolate powder	Low-fat chocolate powder
Chicken	Lean chicken or turkey, skinned; turkey is lowest in fat
Bacon	Leanest bacon you can find; vegetarian bacon
Beef and lamb	Leanest cuts; soya protein
Meat for sandwiches	Lean slices with fat trimmed off; turkey or vegetarian options
Bacon buttie	Toasted bagel with grilled vegetarian sausage, grilled tomato and tomato sauce
Tuna in oil	Tuna in brine
Salmon in oil	Salmon in brine
Eggs	Use three whipped egg whites and one egg yolk
Omelette	Egg white omelette (see page 34)
Fried chips	Oven-baked chips
Potato chips	Pretzels; salted popcorn; low-fat tortilla chips; toasted pitta bread flavoured with seasoning
High-fat fried croutons	Baked croutons
Savoury high-fat snack	Bread sticks
Popcorn	Air pop the corn and simply salt
Creamy mashed potato	Potato flavoured with herbs and mashed with skimmed milk and low-fat yoghurt
Fried fish and chips	Steamed fish with herbs and oven-baked potato chips
Greasy kebab	Grilled lean chicken marinated in a chilli sauce in a pitta pocket with spicy yoghurt topping
Burgers	Chicken or turkey burger, grilled pineapple or peach with extra salad and wholemeal bun
Coconut curry	Low-fat curry (see page 84)
Pizza	Low-fat toppings like vegetables, lean chicken, lean bacon, and lean ham and tomato sauce. Use minimal low-fat cheese. See pages 96.
Soups	Ensure all are made with a vegetable base and the base is puréed. If the soup calls for cream, add skimmed milk, which you can thicken with flour or vegetable purée
Creamy pasta	Use low-fat sauces (see page 104)
Butter on sandwich	Use low-fat mayo in place of butter, or hummus for energy boost
Tuna and mayo sandwich	Low-fat mayo and tuna in brine with added sweetcorn

LUSCIOUS LOW-FAT COOKING

If you are going to cook low-fat then you have to learn which cooking methods are best suited to the recipes in this book. We've all sat down to a fry-up or a roast. The problem is, both these cooking methods retain the fat and, most importantly, it is likely to be bad fat. So you should always remember not only to cut the fat in the way you prepare the food but also in the way you cook it. The cooking methods given below are good because:

1 **They require** little additional fat to aid the cooking process.

2 **They retain** more of the vitamins and minerals in the food.

Remember when your mum used to serve you up boiled carrots and peas and tell you to eat them up because they would make you grow? Well she was only partly right because as most mums boiled the carrots and peas for a long period all the real goodness was boiled out and thrown out with the water.

Grilling

If you grill something correctly then all the fat should drip into the tray. It's the low-fat alternative to a shallow fry-up. Grilling is great for chicken, fish, chicken and vegetables. Ensure you have a grill to place the food on and a tray to catch the fat that drips off naturally. Grilling is also good because you don't need to use fat to initiate the cooking process. In most circumstances you can spray the food with an oil and water combination (see page 27) or use a low-fat basting product or marinade (see opposite).

Luscious advice

- **Char-grilled vegetables are very popular.** Grill a variety of vegetables at the start of the week and use them for sandwich fillings, additions to salads or as an accompaniment to fish and meat.

- **Grilling is the key to a low-fat fry-up.** Cut the fat from the bacon and pop it under the grill together with mushrooms and tomatoes. Select either a low-fat sausage or a vegetarian gourmet sausage. You can fry an egg in a non-stick pan or, if you are feeling virtuous, poach it instead.

Top tips for marinating

- **Marinating adds flavour and spice** – so marinate your meat for a few hours before you grill. Put the meat and marinade mixture in a bowl, cover with plastic wrap and leave in the fridge.

- **Spice up your grilling** marinade with ginger and chilli. Don't throw out the marinade. Use it to baste as you grill.

- **The closer the grill** is to the heat, the quicker it cooks and the more chance it will burn.

- **Oily fish marinate** and grill very well, but white flaky fish don't.

Microwave

How we love this device. It is a fight each night to see who gets to ours first. We have a white one at the moment, but in our cafés there is a stunning silver one that not only microwaves but also grills and bakes – ahh, bliss. Anyway, back to why the microwave is a revolution for the low-fat industry. Well, it's simple. It cooks quickly and through the food without the need to add fat, and we love that.

It's especially good for vegetables. You cut them up, put them in a bowl, add a couple of tablespoons of water, put some microwave film over the top, prick the

Luscious advice

- **If you put fresh asparagus,** baby broccoli stems, courgette slices and green beans into a microwave, within a few minutes you will have a steamed vegetable gourmet meal.

- **If the recipe calls for you to microwave** and it says let the food stand after the machine finishes, then do this. The reason is that the food is still cooking.

film a couple of times and put the bowl in the microwave. Set it for 1 minute, 30 seconds on high and there you go – crisp vegetables in no time. Add some tahini or a salsa and your have a gourmet plate of steamed vegetabes with dips.

Stir-frying

The influence of Eastern cooking on Western cuisine has made stir-frying increasingly popular. The reasons are simple:

- **It's quick.**
- **It's colourful.**
- **It uses less oil.**
- **It allows inexperienced chefs to show off.**

The key to stir-frying is to buy a deep, high quality, non-stick wok. You should also ensure all the food is cut into small pieces to ensure thorough cooking. Stock up on Thai and Chinese cooking oils and marinades to help you to make authentic Asian food at home. Remember that you have to use some oil, but if you follow the golden rule of getting the wok really hot, you'll find things will cook quickly with only a small amount of oil. Products like soy sauce can act as a fat replacement in these circumstances as it is the moisture that aids the cooking.

Luscious advice

- **Pre-cook vegetables** like carrots in the microwave for 30 seconds on high before putting in the microwave.

- **Chilli sauce is great** for adding extra zing to your stir-fry.

- **If you need to add extra oil,** use a spray bottle of half oil and half water (see page 27).

Steaming

Steaming is one of the best low-fat cooking techniques – the steam does the work of fat and the true flavour of what you are cooking is retained. Steaming also makes the colour of the food much more vibrant and retains the vitamins, because there is no water to wash them away. If you are going to steam, you should buy a steamer. Most come with a section for boiling water on the bottom and a cage for the food on top. The boiling water produces steam and cooks the food.

The best foods for steaming are **fish, vegetables, rice** and other grains like barley and s**hell fish.**

Luscious advice

- **When steaming, add fresh herbs** – the steam allows the flavour of the herb to really infuse the food.

- **If you don't have a proper steamer pot,** create your own using a metal basket, hooking it onto the side of a large saucepan and putting hot water underneath.

Boiling

To boil successfully, ensure you cook the vegetables in only a small amount of water, and use the water once the vegetables are taken out to make a gravy or vegetable stock for soup. That you get the benefit of any of the vitamins and nutrients that have boiled out into the water.

Luscious advice

- **Don't over-boil** – ensure the vegetables are crunchy not mushy.

- **Remember that if you over-boil** you will lose up to 70 per cent of the nutrient value of the vegetable.

- **Whenever possible,** choose to steam or microwave your vegetables as this retains their nutrients so much more successfully.

Roasting

Use a roasting tray that has a drip section, then you'll enjoy the benefits of low-fat roasting, which is an excellent way to cook chicken, duck and other fowl as well as meat and some fish. Basting with a low-fat marinade and adding bunches of herbs will add extra flavour. Don't be dainty and cut them up; chuck in large bunches of washed herbs like thyme and rosemary – forget delicate infusions, you want bursts of flavour.

Luscious advice

- **Preparation is the key to good roasting.** Ensure the oven is at roasting temperature and everything is prepared beforehand. A good roast will also make excellent cold meat for lunches.

- **Roasting is great for vegetables** – use a spray of olive oil and water and bunches of rosemary, thyme and garlic to flavour the vegetables you choose (see below).

Over the stove – the good oil

Avoid using butter, fat or oil by going for our fabulous special oil solution. Invest in a good spray bottle (buy a chic stainless steel spray bottle – they look great and work well too), fill it with half olive or other vegetable oil and half water and when you need to use oil, spray with your spray gun instead. You'll be amazed at the results. The spray helps you to get a better coverage on the pan but also means you use less. The key to low-fat cooking is taste, so add taste by including herbs in your oil solution.

The recipes given opposite are some of our particular favourites. To make any – or all – of them, first pour olive oil and water into a spray bottle and then add the other ingredients from the mix of your choice. If you are using chillis, cut them slightly to release their flavour. Once all the ingredients have been added, shake the bottle well and then leave it to rest for at least two weeks in the fridge. Take care when using larger-leaved herbs – they can clog the spray tube, so always shake before use.

HOT to trot

150 ml olive oil
100 ml water
2 garlic cloves, peeled
2 small red chillis

Great for adding flavour to stir-fries and for spraying on food before grilling.

CORIANDER charisma

150 ml olive oil
100 ml water
1 garlic clove, quartered
3 tablespoons light soy sauce
5 sprigs coriander
1 tablespoon runny honey

Excellent for an Asian-style stir-fry and great with fish and chicken dishes. Run the bottle under hot water for 1 minute to make the honey sprayable.

NO thyme to spare

150 ml olive oil
100 ml water
1 garlic clove, peeled and quartered
1 sprig rosemary
1 sprig thyme

Excellent for lamb dishes and for stir-fries with red meats.

BASIL but not faulty

150 ml olive oil
100 ml water
1 garlic clove, quartered
5 sprigs sweet basil

Excellent for spraying through pasta and great for fish dishes.

LUSCIOUS LOW-FAT RECIPES

START THE DAY THE LOW-FAT WAY

You have heard this before and we'll tell you again, breakfast is the most important meal of the day. It literally breaks your overnight fast, hence the name. Traditionally in Britain breakfast has been fat-rich, fry-ups being the most popular option. The problem is, eventually it will kill you. So here we have put together some fantastic breakfast options, which we know you will just love. Pick from pancakes, French toast, fruit compotes, cereals and even low-fat alternatives to fry-ups – and don't forget our fantastic egg white omelettes.

BASIC pancake mixture

Serves 6-8

4 egg whites
300 g self-raising flour
250 ml water
400 ml skimmed milk or buttermilk
100 g caster sugar
2 teaspoons vanilla essence
1 tablespoon olive oil

Nutritional breakdown
(per portion)

Protein 6.4 g
Fat 2.3 g
Sugar 33.4 g
Carbohydrate 61.2 g
Energy 267 k cal

1 Whisk the **egg whites** until fluffy. Mix together the **flour and water** and add the **egg whites** and **all other ingredients** except the **olive oil.**
2 Beat until the **sugar** is dissolved. Heat a non-stick pan and put a small amount of **oil** into the pan. Drop in **2 tablespoons of batter** per pancake. Remember, the pancake is ready to flip when holes appear in the batter on the top.
3 Flip and cook for another 2 minutes and serve.

APPLE-A-DAY pancakes

Serves 4

1 can cooked apples, drained
2 teaspoons cinnamon
1 teaspoon nutmeg

Nutritional breakdown
(per portion)

Protein 13.3 g
Fat 5.4 g
Sugar 72.8 g
Carbohydrate 128.6 g
Energy 579 k cal

1 Mix together the **ingredients** and fold in to the **pancake mixture**.
2 Cook the pancake as above and serve with **a drizzle of honey.**

BANANA and sultana pancakes

Serves 4

100 g brown sugar
3 cloves
2 tablespoons water
8 tablespoons sultanas
3 large bananas, sliced

Nutritional breakdown
(per portion)

Protein 15.0 g
Fat 5.7 g
Sugar 156.5 g
Carbohydrate 214.3 g
Energy 901 k cal

1 Make the pancakes as for the basic recipe, above.
2 Combine the **sugar, cloves and water** in a saucepan and stir until syrupy (you may want to add a **little more water** if the mixture becomes grainy).
3 Bring to the boil and then reduce to simmer. While simmering, add **sultanas and bananas** and gently stir mixture for 5 to 6 minutes.
4 Cool slightly and serve over pancakes.

Luscious advice

- **Replace sultanas** with dried apricots, peaches or prunes for added flavour.

BERRY syrup

Serves 6–8

50 g brown sugar
2 teaspoons rum
1 teaspoon water
200 g selected berries
   (strawberries are best), chopped

Nutritional breakdown
(per portion)

Protein 13.6 g
Fat 4.9 g
Sugar 102.4 g
Carbohydrate 158.2 g
Energy 692 k cal

1 Make the pancakes as for the basic recipe, above.
2 Combine the **sugar, rum and water** and stir until syrupy.
3 Add the **chopped berries** and simmer for approximately 7 minutes or until the consistency resembles puréed fruit.
4 Serve over the pancakes.

Luscious advice

• **Berry inside:** Make the pancake mixture on page 33, adding 200 g chopped berries at the end. Gently fold through and cook. Serve with honey or maple syrup.

SAVOUR the flavour pancake

Serves 6

4 egg whites
500 ml skimmed milk or buttermilk
250 ml water
50 g granulated sugar
2 pinches salt
2 pinches freshly ground black pepper
300 g self-raising flour
1 tablespoon olive oil

Nutritional breakdown
(per portion)

Protein 11.1 g
Fat 2.7 g
Sugar 25.7 g
Carbohydrate 81.4 g
Energy 374 k cal

1 Whisk the **egg whites**. Then mix together all the **other ingredients**, except for the **oil**, and fold in the **egg whites**.
2 Before cooking add any of the extras on page 32 to the batter. We recommend 2 tablespoons per pancake.

FAKE me out bacon pancakes

Serves 6

basic pancake mixture (see page 30)
1 teaspoon olive oil
1 onion, finely chopped
5 tablespoons dried bacon-flavoured bits
(from the dried herb section of
   the supermarket)
2 tablespoons chives

Nutritional breakdown
(per portion)

Protein 8.0 g
Fat 3.2 g
Sugar 34.0 g
Carbohydrate 62.1 g
Energy 294 k cal

1 Heat the **oil** in a non-stick pan and sauté the **chopped onions**. When translucent, drain.
2 Mix the **cooked onions** with the **remaining ingredients** and add to basic savour the flavour pancake mixture.
3 Cook and serve.

BASIC egg white omelette

Serves 4

5 egg whites
salt and freshly ground black pepper
1 teaspoon oil and water spray
  (see page 27)

Nutritional breakdown
(per portion)

Protein 7.5 g
Fat 1.5 g
Sugar 0.0 g
Carbohydrate 0.0 g
Energy 43 k cal

1 Whisk the **egg whites** until they form stiff
peaks. While whisking, add **salt and pepper**, to taste.
2 Put a non-stick pan onto medium heat. Add the **oil and water spray**, warm
through and then add the **egg white mixture**. Gently cook for 2 to 3 minutes.
3 Place the entire pan underneath a heated grill for 1 minute to complete the
cooking process.
4 With an egg-flip, gently fold half the omelette on top of the other half. Serve with
a **small side salad**.

Luscious advice

**Using the egg white omelette as your basic mixture, sprinkle the
following additions onto half of the omelette before placing it under
the grill for 2 minutes.**

- **Hamming it up:** Mix together 4 slices chopped low-fat ham, 1 teaspoon
  grated low-fat cheese and 1 teaspoon thinly chopped chives.

- **Don't chicken out:** Mix together 4 slices chicken or turkey, 1 chopped
  tomato and 2 tablespoons chopped parsley.

- **Chilli outside warm in:** When adding the seasoning, add 1 teaspoon
  finely chopped chilli and 1 teaspoon finely chopped coriander.

BASIC French toast
Serves 4

2 egg whites
150 ml skimmed milk
75 ml low-fat crème fraiche
½ teaspoon vanilla essence
8 slices white bread
60 ml low-fat yoghurt
1 teaspoon honey

Nutritional breakdown
(per portion)

Protein 10.5 g
Fat 1.5 g
Sugar 7.0 g
Carbohydrate 35 g
Energy 187 k cal

1 Beat the **egg whites** until they are peaked, and mix in the **milk, crème fraiche** and **vanilla**.

2 Warm a large non-stick pan.

3 Soak the **slices of bread** in the **egg mixture** and then cook the toast in the frying pan. Brown one side and then the other.

4 Take out of the pan, cut diagonally and serve with a topping of **yoghurt and honey** mixed together.

Luscious variation

- **To make a fruity French toast,** use fruit bread rather than ordinary bread and serve with a delicious topping of fresh strawberries and raspberries.

SAVOURY French Toast

Serves 4

2 egg whites
60 ml quark
8 slices white bread
pinch of salt
pinch of freshly ground black pepper
1 tablespoon bacon-flavoured bits
1 teaspoon of thinly chopped parsley
1 teaspoon of Parmesan cheese
150 ml skimmed milk
tomato relish (see page 67) or salsa
   (see page 63), to serve

Nutritional breakdown
(per portion)

Protein 13.2 g
Fat 3.0 g
Sugar 6.8 g
Carbohydrate 36.0 g
Energy 214 k cal

1 Beat the **egg whites** until they are peaked and then mix in the **remaining ingredients**, except for the **tomato relish or salsa**.
2 While a large non-stick pan is warming through, soak the **slices of fruit bread** in the egg mixture.
3 Cook the toast as before, allowing it to brown on one side before flipping over to the other side.
4 Serve with a topping of **tomato relish** or your **favourite salsa** from this book,

GREEN Asparagus and ham

Serves 4

3 eggs
2 teaspoons grated Parmesan cheese
200 g asparagus, woody ends removed
4 slices low-fat ham
salsa or relish of your choice
   (see pages 62-70)
2 teaspoons parsley or coriander, to serve

Nutritional breakdown
(per portion)

Protein 19.9 g
Fat 9.1 g
Sugar 6.3 g
Carbohydrate 6.6 g
Energy 186 k cal

1 Heat a non-stick frying pan and fry the **eggs**. If you prefer, you can simply poach them.

2 Lay the ham on a baking sheet, sprinkle with half of the **Parmesan cheese** and grill.

3 Steam or microwave the **asparagus**.

4 To serve, lay out the **eggs** and sprinkle with the remaining **Parmesan cheese**. Lay the **asparagus** over the top following by the **ham** and then your **chosen salsa or relish**. Sprinkle with **coriander or parsley**.

SCRAMBLED eggs, salmon and relish

Serves 4

3 organic egg whites
2 organic eggs
60 ml skimmed milk
salt and freshly ground black pepper
2 teaspoons chives
2 bagels
2 tablespoons relish (see pages 67-70)
100 g organic salmon
1 teaspoon parsley, to serve

Nutritional breakdown
(per portion)

Protein 24.4 g
Fat 9.0 g
Sugar 6.1 g
Carbohydrate 47.8 g
Energy 357 k cal

1 In a microwave-proof bowl, whisk the **egg whites** and then beat in the **whole eggs, milk, salt and pepper and chives**.

2 Cover and place in the microwave. Cook on high for 30 seconds, take out and stir gently. Return to the microwave and cook on high for a further 20 seconds, check, stir again and cook for a further 10 seconds. This should be enough, but microwaves differ so you need to test and watch carefully.

3 To serve, toast the **bagels** and cover with **relish**. Then place the **eggs** on top and the **salmon** on top of that, and finally sprinkle with **parsley**.

SULTANA and apple spice

Serves 2

2 tablespoons water
2 apples, chopped
6 tablespoons sultanas
500 ml skimmed milk
250 ml cooked porridge
½ teaspoon cinnamon
2 teaspoons brown sugar

Nutritional breakdown
(per portion)

Protein 9.8 g
Fat 1.8 g
Sugar 49.5 g
Carbohydrate 60.8 g
Energy 282 k cal

1 In a bowl, place **2 tablespoons of water**, the **apples and sultanas**. Cover and heat for 1 ½ minutes in the microwave.
2 Put the **milk** into a saucepan and add the **porridge, cinnamon and sugar**. Bring to the boil and simmer for 1 ½ minutes. Then add the **apple, spice and sultanas mixture**. Stir until cooked and serve.

APRICOT and ginger spice porridge

Serves 2

500 ml skimmed milk
2 tablespoons water
1 cup porridge
½ teaspoon cinnamon
1 x 400 g can apricots, drained
1 teaspoon grated ginger

Nutritional breakdown
(per portion)

Protein 9.5 g
Fat 1.5 g
Sugar 19.7 g
Carbohydrate 28.9 g
Energy 158 k cal

1 Put the **milk and water** into a saucepan and add the **porridge and cinnamon**. Bring to the boil, reduce the heat and simmer for 1 ½ minutes.
2 Add the **apricots and ginger** and stir until cooked and serve.

COMPOTE

Serves 2

250 ml water
8 dried peaches, chopped
8 prunes, chopped
10 dried apples slices, chopped
1 teaspoon orange rind
2 tablespoons walnuts
3 tablespoons honey

Nutritional breakdown
(per portion)

Protein 6.4 g
Fat 7.9 g
Sugar 102.8 g
Carbohydrate 102.9 g
Energy 482 k cal

1 Combine **all the ingredients** in a non-stick pan. Bring to the boil, reduce the heat and simmer for 3 to 6 minutes.
2 Remember you can add to and change the fruits you use. Try **dates, sultanas, raisins or dried tropical fruit**.

SOUPS

Soups are great. They are filling and warming, and we often drink them like tea or coffee – plus if made using the right ingredients they are low in fat. The thing we like about soup is that you can experiment so easily.

These soups are not about wasting time. Basically, it's a chuck it all in and purée approach. They are both low-fat and ready in no time. Here are some basics that Tony and I like.

BASIC vegetable soup

Serves 4

500 ml water
2 onions, chopped
4 carrots, chopped
1 parsnip, chopped
10 mushrooms, chopped
3 sticks of celery, chopped
4 potatoes, chopped
1 leek, chopped
1 x 400 g can chopped tomatoes
2 sprigs fresh thyme, chopped
salt and freshly ground black pepper
2 cloves garlic, chopped

Nutritional breakdown
(per portion)

Protein 5.5 g
Fat 1.7 g
Sugar 13.3 g
Carbohydrate 28.3 g
Energy 143 k cal

1 Put **all ingredients** into a large non-stick pan and bring to the boil. Reduce the heat and simmer for 2 hours, stirring occasionally.
2 You can then serve the soup with chunks or blend it in a food processor. If you want to make a creamier version, add **250 ml low-fat yoghurt** when you blend.
3 To make a **low-fat stock**, strain the soup once it is cooked.

CARROT and sweetcorn chowder

Serves 4

1 red onion, chopped
1 white onion, chopped
oil spray
1-2 gloves garlic, chopped
½ teaspoon chilli powder
8 medium carrots, chopped
250 ml vegetable stock
salt and freshly ground black pepper
8 medium potatoes, chopped
2 x 400 g cans sweetcorn, drained
250 ml skimmed evaporated milk

Nutritional breakdown
(per portion)

Protein 11.8 g
Fat 2.6 g
Sugar 20.2 g
Carbohydrate 54.0 g
Energy 273 k cal

1 Sauté the **onions** in the pan using a **little oil spray**. Add the **garlic and chilli powder** (you can use **fresh chilli**) to release the flavours.

2 Add the **carrots, vegetable stock and salt and pepper** to taste and cook until the **carrots** are crisp.

3 In the meantime, put the **potatoes** into a separate pan and cook until they are soft. Drain the water and combine the **potatoes** and the contents of the **vegetable mixture** with the **sweetcorn and evaporated milk**. Re-heat and simmer until all **vegetables** are tender (approximately 10 minutes).

4 And now for the secret bit. Take half the mixture, purée it and it return to the chowder. Heat again and serve.

Luscious advice

- **Replace carrots** with courgettes, pumpkin or sweet potato.

- **For a more corny flavour,** double the amount of sweetcorn and cut back on the potatoes.

TOMATO soup

Serves 4

2 red onions, chopped
12 garlic cloves, crushed
2 sticks celery, chopped
spray oil
15 medium vine ripened tomatoes, chopped
  or 4 x 400 g cans chopped tomatoes, drained
10 basil leaves, chopped
400 ml vegetable stock or water
salt and freshly ground black pepper

Nutritional breakdown
(per portion)

Protein 17.5 g
Fat 1.1 g
Sugar 11.7 g
Carbohydrate 19.6 g
Energy 113 k cal

1 Sauté the **onions, garlic and celery** in a pan in **some spray oi**l. Add the **tomatoes** and cook for 4 minutes.
2 Add the **chopped basil leaves, vegetable stock or water** and season to taste. Bring to the boil, reduce the heat and simmer for 40 minutes.
3 Transfer the mixture to a food processor, blend to a purée and serve.

Luscious advice

• **For a creamy texture,** replace half the vegetable stock with the same amount of skimmed evaporated milk or low-fat yoghurt.

LOW-FAT minestrone

Serves 4

1 onion, chopped
spray oil
1 litre vegetable stock
3 teaspoons Italian seasoning mix
5 tablespoons tomato purée
3 medium carrots, chopped
2 medium potatoes, chopped
3 medium tomatoes, chopped
2 medium parsnips, chopped
4 handfuls pasta twirls
2 handfuls spinach
2 handfuls chopped cabbage
250 ml water
¼ teaspoon freshly ground black pepper

Nutritional breakdown
(per portion)

Protein 8.0 g
Fat 5.8 g
Sugar 18.2 g
Carbohydrate 34.4 g
Energy 210 k cal

1 In a pan, sauté the **onion** in a **little spray oil** and then add **125 ml of the stock** and the **dried herbs** and cook for 2 to 3 minutes. Add the **remaining stock, tomato purée and all the vegetables** except for the **spinach and cabbage**.
2 Bring to the boil, reduce the heat and simmer for 1 hour 20 minutes, adding water as necessary.
3 Before serving, heat again and add the **pasta**. Boil until the **pasta** is just ready and then add the **cabbage and spinach** and cook for a further 3 minutes. This should leave the **cabbage and spinach** just crunchy enough. Season to taste.

Luscious advice

- **If you don't have** Italian seasoning mix, make your own with ½ teaspoon each of dried thyme, basil and oregano.

- **Try adding** butter beans for additional flavour.

LOW-FAT luscious Thai inspired noodle soup

Serves 4

300 g skinless chicken breast, thinly sliced
oil and water spray (see page 27)
1 onion, finely chopped
2 cloves garlic, finely chopped
2 teaspoons finely chopped fresh ginger
2 teaspoons turmeric
400 ml low-fat evaporated milk
½ teaspoon coconut essence
250 ml low-fat chicken stock
10 button mushrooms, thinly sliced
500 g hokkien noodles or spaghetti
100 g mangetout
1 handful bean sprouts
4 tablespoons finely chopped
   coriander leaves

Nutritional breakdown
(per portion)

Protein 26.1 g
Fat 6.9 g
Sugar 3.4 g
Carbohydrate 24.4 g
Energy 258 k cal

1 Brown the **chicken pieces** in a pan using a small amount of **oil and water spray**.
2 At the same time, spray a large, heavy-based pan with **oil**. Add the **onion** and cook over medium heat for 2 minutes. Add the **garlic, ginger and turmeric** and stir-fry for a further 30 seconds.
3 Gradually add the **evaporated milk**, **coconut essence** and **stock**, stirring to scrape the **onion and spices** from the bottom. Bring to the boil, reduce the heat, and add the **chicken and mushrooms**. Simmer for a further 2 to 3 minutes.
4 Add the **noodles** and heat through. Divide the soup and noodles between four bowls and top with **mangetout, sprouts and coriander**.

LOW-FAT prawn laksa

Serves

3 tablespoons shrimp or fish paste
1 medium red onion, chopped
3 small red chillies
2 large garlic cloves, crushed
spray oil
500 ml low-fat evaporated milk
½ teaspoon coconut essence
400 ml low-fat chicken stock
450 g large green prawns
1 handful bean sprouts
250 g rice noodles or
   500 g fresh laksa noodles
8 tablespoons fresh coriander leaves
6 shallots, thinly sliced

Nutritional breakdown
(per portion)

Protein 28.8 g
Fat 8.7 g
Sugar 4.3 g
Carbohydrate 58.2 g
Energy 432 k cal

1 Place the **paste, onion, chilli and garlic** in a heavy-based pan with a **little spray** oil and cook over medium heat, stirring constantly for 2 minutes.
2 Add the **evaporated milk, coconut essence and stock** and stir to combine. Bring to the boil over a high heat. Reduce heat to medium-low and simmer, partially covered, for 5 minutes.
3 Add the **prawns** to the soup and cook for 1 to 2 minutes or until they curl and change colour. Add the **bean sprouts** and cook for a further minute.
4 Meanwhile, add the **rice noodles** to a medium saucepan of boiling water and cook for 3 minutes or until tender. Drain and divide among four bowls.
5 Place the **coriander and green shallots** into serving bowls with the **noodles** and ladle the hot soup over the top. Serve immediately.

Luscious variation

- **If you don't like prawns,** try fish laksa. Instead of prawns used 450 g salmon chunks or your favourite fish.

SALADS

We love salads because they are easy to make and are a fantastic way to get your proper daily intake of fruit and vegetables. We've taken salads to a new dimension. Instead of sticking to traditional concepts, we like to mix and match flavours and give the palate a chance to enjoy a range of tastes.

The best thing about salads is that they are easy to make … so you can spend your time eating not making. We start with some traditional favourites designed to be low in fat.

CAESAR salad

Serves 6

1 Cos lettuce
3 slices bread (brown, white or ciabatta, whatever you have)
spray oil
½ teaspoon garlic salt
freshly ground black pepper
4 vine-ripened tomatoes or 10 cherry tomatoes, chopped
1 egg
30 cm cucumber, roughly chopped
4 tablespoons olives
½ red onion, sliced (optional)
4 tablespoons grated low-fat cheese
1 egg, hard-boiled, shelled and quartered

DRESSING
2 tablespoons lemon juice
½ teaspoon freshly ground black pepper
2 cloves garlic, finely chopped
125 ml low-fat sour cream
125 ml skimmed milk
2 tablespoons Dijon mustard
salt

Nutritional breakdown
(per portion)

Protein 6.7 g
Fat 3.7 g
Sugar 3.5 g
Carbohydrate 10.2 g
Energy 98 k cal

1 Wash the **lettuce** and rip or chop leaves and then leave to dry. Chop the **bread** into small cubes.

2 Heat some **oil spray** in a non-stick pan and add the **cubed bread**. Sprinkle with **garlic salt and pepper** and cook for 5 minutes. Turn the **bread** and cook for another 5 minutes until browned all over.

3 For the dressing, place **all the ingredients** into a bowl and mix. If you prefer, you can place them into a food processor and blend for 20 to 30 seconds.

4 Place **lettuce leaves** into a bowl and cover with **125 ml dressing** and mix. I prefer to use my hands for this.

5 Then add the **chopped tomatoes, cucumber, olives** and, if you like, **a few slivers of sliced red onion**.

6 If you wish, add a **little more dressing** and then sprinkle with **cheese** and top with the **croutons and quartered egg**.

Luscious advice

- **For added flavour** to your dressing, mix in 2 teaspoons of bacon-flavoured bits. These are made with soya and are low in fat.

- **Some people** prefer meat with their salad. If so, add 100 g skinned and chopped lean chicken or turkey.

- **Or take 8 slices of chopped low-fat ham** and grill for 3 to 4 minutes and mix through. The grilling crisps the ham for some added crunch.

TUNA Niçoise

Serves 6

1 large handful green beans
2 heads coloured lettuce
1 red onion, chopped
15 cm cucumber, roughly chopped
10 cherry tomatoes, chopped in half
1 x 400 g can tuna in brine, drained
4 tablespoons olives in brine
10 new potatoes, cooked
2 eggs, hard-boiled, shelled and quartered
4 tablespoons good quality vinegar
2 teaspoons parsley

Nutritional breakdown
(per portion)

Protein 15.5 g
Fat 3.7 g
Sugar 2.9 g
Carbohydrate 10.3 g
Energy 133 k cal

1 Steam the **beans** until just crisp and then leave to cool.
2 Meanwhile, wash the **lettuce leaves** and rip. Place on the base of a salad bowl. Scatter the **red onions, cucumber and tomatoes** over the top. Then place the **tuna** in the centre.
3 If you'd like to be artistic, lay the **beans** around the **tuna** together with the **olives** and new potatoes. Add the quartered eggs. Drizzle with vinegar and sprinkle with parsley. Serve.

Luscious advice

- **For extra kick** use a flavoured vinegar.

- **You can also** use salmon instead of tuna.

PEACHY keen

Serves 2

2 heads coloured lettuce
1 handful bean sprouts
3 fresh peaches
100 g low-fat ricotta cheese
5 slices low-fat ham, roughly chopped
3 tablespoons parsley
red wine vinaigrette
salt and freshly ground black pepper

Nutritional breakdown
(per portion)

Protein 22.6 g
Fat 4.3 g
Sugar 14.6 g
Carbohydrate 15.5 g
Energy 186 k cal

1 This is easy. First, wash and dry the **lettuce leaves** and lay them on a large serving dish.
2 Sprinkle with the **sprouts**.
3 Wash the **peaches**, roughly rip apart and add to the **lettuce and sprouts**.
4 To serve, place the **ricotta** around the dish and place the **chopped ham** over the salad. Sprinkle with **parsley** and drizzle with **vinaigrette**. Add **salt and pepper**, to taste.

Luscious advice

This fruity salad works well with the following combinations.

- **Replace peaches** with fresh mangoes.

- **Replace peaches** with fresh apricots.

- **Replace peaches** with fresh strawberries.

- **For a more savoury style salad,** replace peaches with sun-ripened tomatoes rehydrated in water.

POTATO salad

Serves 6

1 kg baby potatoes, boiled in their skins
2 large red onions, finely chopped
1 x 400 g can sweetcorn, drained
8 tablespoons chopped flat parsley
1 stick celery, chopped

DRESSING
250 ml low-fat yoghurt
125 ml skimmed milk
1 garlic clove, crushed
2 teaspoons sugar
freshly ground black pepper
2 tablespoons lemon juice

Nutritional breakdown
(per portion)

Protein 7.2 g
Fat 1.8 g
Sugar 10.0 g
Carbohydrate 37.8 g
Energy 186 k cal

1 Make the dressing by placing **all the ingredients** in a food processor and blending for 30 seconds.
2 Place all the **salad ingredients** into a bowl, stir through the **dressing** and serve.

Luscious variations

- **Chop 2 chillies** and mix through the salad to add some kick.

- **For a protein fix,** chop up 100 g of lean turkey or ham and sprinkle over the top of the completed salad.

- **Add** 50 g bacon-flavoured bits for extra crunch.

- **For an unusual combination,** replace the parsley with basil – this will give your salad a more exotic taste.

BASIC coleslaw

Serves 6

½ small green cabbage, finely sliced
½ small red cabbage, finely sliced
6 medium carrots, grated
1 red onion, sliced
2 stick celery, chopped
3 tablespoons sultanas

DRESSING
3 tablespoons low-fat mayonnaise

Nutritional breakdown
(per portion)

Protein 5.1 g
Fat 1.1 g
Sugar 34.0 g
Carbohydrate 35.7 g
Energy 165 k cal

1 Mix together **all the ingredients**.
2 Add the **dressing** and mix through.

ASIAN-STYLE variation

Serves 6

1 quantity basic coleslaw recipe
2 handfuls bean sprouts
4 tablespoons chopped coriander
8 tablespoons chopped pineapple

DRESSING
3 tablespoons low-fat lemon
    or lime mayonnaise

Nutritional breakdown
(per portion)

Protein 6.0 g
Fat 1.3 g
Sugar 38.1 g
Carbohydrate 40.2 g
Energy 187 k cal

1 Mix together **all the ingredients**.
2 Add the **mayonnaise** and stir through.

ITALIAN variation

Serves 6

1 quantity basic coleslaw recipe
8 tablespoons chopped drained black and green olives
4 tablespoons chopped basil
½ pepper, deseeded and chopped
1 small courgette, grated

DRESSING
250 ml vinaigrette
125 ml tomato juice
1 teaspoon sugar
½ tablespoon freshly ground black pepper

Nutritional breakdown
(per portion)

Protein 6.3 g
Fat 2.1 g
Sugar 37.1 g
Carbohydrate 39.0 g
Energy 190 k cal

1 Mix together **all the ingredients**.
2 Make the **dressing** by mixing together **all the ingredients** and stir through the salad.

PUMPKIN and mint variation

Serves 6

1 quantity basic recipe
100 g grated pumpkin
125 g grated sweet potatoes
20 g chopped mint
125 g low-fat mayonnaise

Nutritional breakdown
(per portion)

Protein 5.8 g
Fat 1.3 g
Sugar 38.1 g
Carbohydrate 42.9 g
Energy 196 k cal

1 Mix together **all the ingredients**.

BASIC wild rice salad

Serves 6

200 g cooked wild rice
½ red pepper, deseeded and chopped
½ yellow pepper, deseeded and chopped
1 x 400 g can sweetcorn
3 medium tomatoes, chopped
1 stick celery, chopped
6 tablespoons sultanas
4 tablespoons chopped basil

DRESSING
3 tablespoons cider vinegar
1 tablespoon olive oil
1 teaspoon lemon juice
2 tablespoons chopped fresh parsley
1 tablespoon sugar
salt and freshly ground black pepper

Nutritional breakdown
(per portion)

Protein 5.4 g
Fat 2.7 g
Sugar 25.4 g
Carbohydrate 59.3 g
Energy 269 k cal

1 For the salad, combine **all ingredients**.
2 For the dressing, mix **all the ingredients** and combine with the **salad**.

Luscious variations

- **Make the basic wild rice salad** but replace the basil with coriander and add 1 handful bean sprouts, 2 handfuls thinly sliced Chinese cabbage and ½ teaspoon of chilli. In the dressing, replace the lemon juice with 1 tablespoon soy sauce.

- **Adding some blueberries** to the basic wild rice salad instead of sultanas makes an unusual taste sensation.

To make each of the recipes on these pages, simply gather up the listed ingredients, toss together in a bowl and serve.

THAI twist chunky chilli

Serves 8

500 g pre-cooked and cooled chickpeas
    or 3 x 400 g cans chickpeas, drained
1 medium chilli, deseeded and roughly
    chopped
5 tablespoons crumbled feta
8 tablespoons roughly chopped coriander,
    chives and parsley in equal portions
2 red onions, sliced into rings
125 ml cider vinegar or vinegar flavoured
    with coriander or chillies
salt and freshly ground black pepper

Nutritional breakdown
(per portion)

Protein 6.75 g
Fat 2.45 g
Sugar 2.4 g
Carbohydrate 13.6 g
Energy 100 k cal

PUMPKIN seeds with watermelon and rock melon

Serves 8

500 g chopped, deseeded watermelon
8 tablespoons pumpkin seeds
grated rind of 2 lemons
juice of 2 lemons or limes

Nutritional breakdown
(per portion)

Protein 1.45 g
Fat 2.2 g
Sugar 4.55 g
Carbohydrate 5.2 g
Energy 44.5 k cal

GINGER cabbage

Serves 6

2 handfuls chopped red cabbage
2 handfuls chopped green cabbage
2 handfuls chopped white cabbage
300 g grapes
4 tablespoons roughly chopped coriander
3 tablespoons grated fresh ginger
4 tablespoons almonds, walnuts or mixed
  nuts, finely chopped in food processor
250 ml vinegar flavoured with raspberries
  or coriander

Nutritional breakdown
(per portion)

Protein 2.0 g
Fat 2.3 g
Sugar 8.6 g
Carbohydrate 9.2 g
Energy 68 k cal

ASPARAGUS and tomatoes

Serves 6

3 large handfuls asparagus, steamed,
  cooled and chopped
8 vine-ripened cherry tomatoes, chopped
1 large red onion, chopped
3 radishes, chopped
8 tablespoons equal quantities roughly
  chopped parsley and basil
125 ml balsamic vinegar
8 large strawberries or 1 peeled and chopped
  mango or equivalent quantity of whatever
fruit you choose

Nutritional breakdown
(per portion)

Protein 1.2 g
Fat 0.3 g
Sugar 4.2 g
Carbohydrate 4.6 g
Energy 25 k cal

SANDWICHES

When it comes to the lunch hour, new research has shown that most people have around 25 minutes to eat, and even that is usually spent running messages, doing errands or shopping. That means we usually grab a sandwich – whatever we can find – and stuff it in our mouths. This is just not healthy – for two reasons:

- The choice on the high street is limited, so you often end up eating high-fat because it is more readily available.
- You eat on the run and this can be disruptive. Personal time to eat is essential.

Here we start with the basics – butter replacers. Low-fat mayonnaise is fantastic. Our mayonnaise alternatives are also great as salad dressings or with jacket potatoes. An alternative to mayonnaise is a combination of half low-fat yoghurt and half sour cream. Our mayonnais recipes come in two options. Choose the option that suits you and add the flavours.

- Option 1: 250 ml your favourite low-fat mayo
- Option 2: 250 ml low-fat yoghurt mixed with 2 tablespoons of quark

We all love sandwich fillings that are chunky and filling. There is a misconception that a low-fat sandwich must be slim and tiny – you know, the cucumber with no crust type. That's rubbish and these recipes prove it. Here are some chunky sandwich fillings that are great for:

- Sandwiches.
- Open sandwiches.
- Pitta bread pockets.
- Wraps.

For truly delicious sandwich fillings mix together the ingredients from any of the following recipes – it only takes about 30 seconds.

LEMON low-fat mayo

Serves 8

Option 1 or 2 and add:
2 tablespoons freshly squeezed lemon juice
freshly ground black pepper

> **Nutritional breakdown**
> (per portion)
>
> Protein 1.65 g
> Fat 0.5 g
> Sugar 2.4 g
> Carbohydrate 2.4 g
> Energy 18 k cal

LIME low-fat mayo

Serves 4

Option 1 or 2 and add:
2 tablespoons freshly squeezed lime juice
freshly ground black pepper

> **Nutritional breakdown**
> (per portion)
>
> Protein 3.3 g
> Fat 0.5 g
> Sugar 4.8 g
> Carbohydrate 4.8 g
> Energy 36 k cal

SALSA mayonnaise

Serves 4

Option 1 or 2 and add:
250 ml salsa (see page 63)
1 tablespoon lemon juice
1 teaspoon chopped chilli

> **Nutritional breakdown**
> (per portion)
>
> Protein 3.5 g
> Fat 0.6 g
> Sugar 5.3 g
> Carbohydrate 5.5 g
> Energy 40 k cal

CRANBERRY mayonnaise

Serves 4

Option 1 or 2 (see page 56)
2 tablespoons cranberry sauce or jelly

Nutritional breakdown
(per portion)

Protein 3.8 g
Fat 1.1 g
Sugar 5.4 g
Carbohydrate 5.6 g
Energy 46 k cal

MUSTARD mayo

Serves 4

Option 1 or 2 (see page 56)
2 tablespoons mustard
1 teaspoon horseradish

Nutritional breakdown
(per portion)

Protein 3.2 g
Fat 0.5 g
Sugar 4.8 g
Carbohydrate 4.8 g
Energy 35 k cal

SEXY chilli mayo

Serves 4

Option 1 or 2 (see page 56)
1 teaspoon chopped chilli
1 teaspoon garlic paste

Nutritional breakdown
(per portion)

Protein 31.4 g
Fat 2.8 g
Sugar 5.7 g
Carbohydrate 42.9 g
Energy 311 k cal

Luscious variations

• **Low-fat mayonnaise** is a great base for different added flavours. Try mint, dill, chives and basil. This can change the taste of your mayonnaise and give your meal a kick.

CHILLI tuna sandwich

Serves 2

4 tablespoons sexy chilli mayonnaise
 (see opposite)
2 large coloured lettuce leaves
185 g can tuna flakes in brine
10 cm celery, finely chopped
salt and freshly ground black pepper
6 bread slices

Nutritional breakdown
(per portion)

Protein 10.8 g
Fat 3.7 g
Sugar 3.3 g
Carbohydrate 4.4 g
Energy 92 k cal

1 Spread the **bread slices** with a light smearing of the **chilli mayonnaise** and top
with **lettuce leaf**.
2 Mix the **remaining mayonnaise** with other the ingredients and serve as an
open-topped sandwich.

Luscious variations

- **This recipe can be altered** by simply changing the mayonnaise
  mix you use. Try lime mayonnaise or lemon mayonnaise or, for a
  Mexican style lunch, try the salsa mayo.

LOW-FAT herbed eggs

Serves 2

1 hard-boiled egg, finely chopped
whites of 3 other boiled eggs, finely chopped
2 tablespoons finely chopped parsley
1 tablespoon chives
2 tablespoons mustard mayo
freshly ground black pepper
1 handful beansprouts, chopped

Nutritional breakdown
(per portion)

Protein 8.3 g
Fat 3.9 g
Sugar 3.5 g
Carbohydrate 19.8 g
Energy 142 k cal

1 Combine all the **ingredients**. The chunkiness of the mixture depends on how finely you chop the **egg**.
2 Serve using a smearing of **low-fat mayonnaise** on the bread.

For each of the following recipes, mix together all the ingredients and pop between two slices of your favourite bread.

CHUNKY post-Christmas turkey crunch

Serves 2

200 g low-fat lean turkey, chopped
4 tablespoons cranberry mayonnaise
1 small red onion, finely chopped
2 tablespoons chopped walnuts

Nutritional breakdown
(per portion)

Protein 14.2 g
Fat 2.2 g
Sugar 1.4 g
Carbohydrate 1.4 g
Energy 82 k cal

LEMON Thai chicken chunks

Serves 4

100 g low-fat chicken, chopped
4 tablespoons lemon low-fat mayonnaise
10 cm celery, chopped
2 tablespoons chopped coriander
1 teaspoon chopped chilli

Nutritional breakdown

(per portion)

Protein 14.2 g
Fat 2.2 g
Sugar 1.4 g
Carbohydrate 1.4 g
Energy 82 k cal

SPRING into summer

Serves 4

3 carrots, grated
1 handful beansprouts
½ apple, grated
2 teaspoons sesame seeds
2 tablespoons chopped walnuts
1 handful chopped baby spinach
200 g low-fat cottage cheese
1 red onion, chopped
1 tablespoon chopped parsley

Nutritional breakdown

(per portion)

Protein 8.1 g
Fat 4.6 g
Sugar 10.6 g
Carbohydrate 11.8 g
Energy 118 k cal

CHUNKY ham and sun-dried tomato

Serves 2

8 slices low-fat ham, chopped
8 rehydrated sun-dried tomatoes, chopped
1 tablespoon chopped parsley
4 tablespoons chopped pineapple
1 tablespoon chives
250 g low-fat cottage cheese

Nutritional breakdown

(per portion)

Protein 33.3 g
Fat 5.2 g
Sugar 14.9 g
Carbohydrate 15.0 g
Energy 235 k cal

SAUCES, DIPS AND CRISPS

Salsas and sauces, relishes and toppings are essential to our low-fat lifestyle. The reasons are simple:

- They can replace butter on sandwiches.
- They make a sandwich interesting.
- They add zing to salad.
- They add zap to meat.
- They add the decadent indulgence we associate with high-fat foods.
- They simply taste great.

We suggest that you make up the salad dressings, mayos, sauces and salsas that you like and keep them in the refrigerator. Your friends will also adore them.

A salsa is a combination of vegetables and sometimes fruit, usually with vinegar, lime, lemon or oil added to combine the flavours. Traditionally they are used on tacos but, hey, we use them on everything from fish to sandwiches and they make great low-fat dips, especially for parties, when you can offer a range of the salsas given here.

To make the salsas on these pages, simply mix all the ingredients in a bowl and serve or store in a jar in the refrigerator.

Everyone loves chips. They are a fantastic snack, they make you feel great when you have an energy low and we've grown up with them. The trouble is that high-fat chips mean big hips. So we've developed a system that allows you to make snack chips to take with you to help with those cravings or to offer at parties. We call these gourmet slim hip crisps.

They make great party food. Beetroot, sweet potato, pumpkin and carrot are all strong flavours and people will be amazed at how low in fat they are. For a snack attack, mix up your crisps and pack them into small airtight bags so you can grab a bag or two each morning. They also make fab fun gifts if you put them into clear cellophane bags and tie them with a red ribbon.

BASIC tomato salsa

Serves 4

1 x 400 g can chopped tomatoes
  or 5 vine-ripened tomatoes, chopped
2 cloves garlic, crushed
1 red onion, chopped
1 red pepper, deseeded and chopped
1 tablespoon chopped basil or parsley

Nutritional breakdown
(per portion)

Protein 2.1 g
Fat 0.3 g
Sugar 5.1 g
Carbohydrate 7.2 g
Energy 38 k cal

PINING for me salsa

Serves 4 to 6

300 g chopped fresh pineapple
1 small red onion, chopped
1 green pepper, deseeded and chopped
1 small chilli pepper, deseeded and chopped
2 tablespoons orange juice
3 tablespoons finely chopped coriander
3 tablespoons of vinegar

Nutritional breakdown
(per portion)

Protein 1.2 g
Fat 0.3 g
Sugar 6.9 g
Carbohydrate 7.2 g
Energy 35 k cal

MANGO and watermelon salsa

Serves 4

300 g watermelon, deseeded and chopped
1 mango, peeled, pitted and chopped
4 tablespoons chopped chives
1 green pepper, deseeded and chopped
1 medium jalapeno chilli pepper,
  deseeded and finely chopped (optional)
1 tablespoon fresh lime juice

Nutritional breakdown
(per portion)

Protein 1.5 g
Fat 0.5 g
Sugar 12.5 g
Carbohydrate 12.7 g
Energy 58 k cal

MIXED pepper salsa

Serves 4

1 red pepper, deseeded and chopped
1 yellow pepper, deseeded and chopped
1 green pepper, deseeded and chopped
2 tablespoons chopped red onion
2 small vine-ripened tomatoes, chopped
½ tablespoon vinegar
2 tablespoons chopped parsley
salt and freshly ground black pepper

Nutritional breakdown
(per portion)

Protein 1.4 g
Fat 0.5 g
Sugar 4.9 g
Carbohydrate 5.3 g
Energy 29 k cal

CUCUMBER salsa

Serves 4

30 cm chopped cucumber
1 small red onion, chopped
1 red pepper, deseeded and chopped
1 radish, chopped
1 tablespoon Tabasco sauce
1 tablespoon sherry vinegar
2 tablespoons parsley, coriander and
  basil mixed together

Nutritional breakdown
(per portion)

Protein 1.2 g
Fat 0.3 g
Sugar 3.8 g
Carbohydrate 4.5 g
Energy 25 k cal

PUMPKIN and carrot dip

Serves 4

500 g butternut pumpkin, peeled and chopped
6 medium carrots, chopped
3 tablespoons quark
3 cloves garlic
½ tablespoon vinegar
3 tablespoons cumin seeds or sesame seeds
salt and freshly ground black pepper
1 handful parsley, chopped, to serve

> **Nutritional breakdown**
> (per portion)
>
> Protein 11.9 g
> Fat 2.2 g
> Sugar 2.9 g
> Carbohydrate 4.2 g
> Energy 83 k cal

1 Boil the **pumpkin and carrots** until soft (approximately 15-20 minutes) and drain. I prefer to steam in microwave for 5-10 minutes as this keeps in nutrients.
2 Put **all the ingredients** into a mixing bowl and mash through until soft. Alternatively, blend in a food processor.
3 Serve with **a sprinkle of parsley**.

BACON or ham dip

Serves 4

4 rashers grilled lean bacon
  or 4 slices low-fat ham
4 tablespoons chopped chives
250 ml plain low-fat yoghurt or quark
6 tablespoons low-fat mayonnaise
¼ teaspoon paprika
8 drops Tabasco sauce
2 cloves garlic, crushed

> **Nutritional breakdown**
> (per portion)
>
> Protein 5.0 g
> Fat 2.7 g
> Sugar 11.0 g
> Carbohydrate 14.0 g
> Energy 77 k cal

1 Grill the **bacon** and place between two layers of paper towel to absorb **excess oil**. Chop into small pieces. If you are using **low-fat ham, simply chop it**.
2 In a separate bowl, thoroughly mix the **remaining ingredients** and then fold in the **ham or bacon**. Allow to cool in the refrigerator for half a day and serve.

GREEN pea guacamole

Serves 4

400 g cooked fresh green peas
1 tablespoon low-fat cream cheese
2 tablespoons low-fat sour cream
2 teaspoons lime or lemon juice
1 teaspoon fresh chilli
1 tablespoon tomato purée
few drops Tabasco sauce

Nutritional breakdown
(per portion)

Protein 8.2 g
Fat 1.5 g
Sugar 3.2 g
Carbohydrate 10.0 g
Energy 83 k cal

1 Place **all the ingredients** except for the **Tabasco sauce** into a food processor and blend until smooth.
2 Add **Tabasco** to taste. Refrigerate until required.

CRAB or salmon or tuna dip

Serves 4

250 ml low-fat yoghurt or quark
2 tablespoons low-fat mayonnaise
1 tablespoon skimmed milk
½ teaspoon dry mustard
100 g cottage cheese
⅛ teaspoon paprika
1 tablespoon horseradish
¼ teaspoon Tabasco sauce
400 g crab, tuna, salmon, haddock or lobster
  (either fresh or in brine from a can – different
  seafoods have different fat quantities)

Nutritional breakdown
(per portion)

Protein 5.0 g
Fat 2.7 g
Sugar 11.0 g
Carbohydrate 14.0 g
Energy 77 k cal

1 If using **fresh fish**, steam until cooked and then flake. Set to one side.
2 Place **all the ingredients** except the **seafood** into a food processor. Pulse for 1 minute until chunky but not creamy.
3 Place in bowl and fold in the **flaked seafood**, cool and serve.

LOW-FAT sun-dried tomato dip

Serves 4

10 chopped rehydrated sun-dried tomatoes
250 ml of low-fat cottage cheese
2 tablespoons chopped coriander
1 tablespoon tomato puree
salt and freshly ground black pepper

Nutritional breakdown
(per portion)

Protein 9.3 g
Fat 1.2 g
Sugar 4.8 g
Carbohydrate 4.9 g
Energy 65 k cal

1 Place **all the ingredients** in a food processor
and blend for 2 minutes. Check the texture and
if necessary blend for a further 1 minute. Season to taste.
2 If you prefer the chunky approach, hand mix the ingredients. The chunky
variation makes a good side dish on a buffet and is rich in calcium.

TOMATO relish

Serves 4

1 red onion
olive oil and basil mix (see page 27)
1 tablespoon brown sugar
4 medium tomatoes, chopped
freshly ground black pepper
2 tablespoons balsamic vinegar

Nutritional breakdown
(per portion)

Protein 0.8 g
Fat 0.2 g
Sugar 8.2 g
Carbohydrate 8.6 g
Energy 36 k cal

1 Cook the **onions** in a non-stick pan in **olive oil and basil,** mixing, until brown.
2 Add the **brown sugar and tomatoes**, stirring until all the flavours have
intermingled.
3 Add **seasoning and vinegar** and then leave to cool. Store in a jar in the
refrigerator.

ITALIAN relish

Serves 4

2 red onions, chopped
1 red onion, finely chopped
2 teaspoons olive oil and chilli spray
  (see page 27)
4 large tomatoes, chopped
4 tablespoons chopped ripe olives
1 tablespoon fresh lime juice
1 tablespoon lemon juice
4 teaspoons chopped fresh
  or 1 teaspoon dried oregano
2 cloves garlic, finely chopped
salt and freshly ground black pepper

Nutritional breakdown
(per portion)

Protein 1.9 g
Fat 3.1 g
Sugar 3.8 g
Carbohydrate 7.8 g
Energy 65 k cal

1 Sauté the **onions** in a non-stick pan in **olive oil and chilli mix**. Then add the **tomatoes** and cook for 5 minutes until hot and combined.
2 Mix in **all the other ingredients** and cook for a further 10 minutes on a medium heat. Cool and place in a jar.

Luscious variations

• **Adding chilli** to any relish recipe will spice it up. A good relish can also make a great glaze for a roast or for barbecuing a lean piece of chicken or beef.

• **Instead of** the pineapple chunks, use mango.

• **Experiment with flavours.** Start with the basic onion or tomato relish and add to that. Don't be afraid to mix your flavours.

COLOURED bean relish

Serves 4–8

2 onions, chopped
100 g black beans, rinsed and drained
100 g red beans
100 g sweetcorn
2 tablespoons deseeded and chopped
 green pepper
2 tablespoons chopped tomato
1 tablespoon chopped chives
1 tablespoon chopped parsley
1 tablespoon lemon juice
1 teaspoon olive oil
¼ teaspoon ground cumin
salt and freshly ground black pepper

Nutritional breakdown
(per portion)

Protein 12.7 g
Fat 2.9 g
Sugar 2.6 g
Carbohydrate 26.0 g
Energy 172 k cal

1 Fry the **onions** in a non-stick pan.
2 Combine **all the ingredients** in a bowl.
3 Serve the relish chilled or at room temperature.

PEA and corn relish

Serves 4

1 x 400 g can sweetcorn, drained
300 g peas, steamed
2 tablespoons lime juice
1 tablespoon extra virgin olive oil
2 tablespoons balsamic vinegar
2 tablespoons chopped red onion
½ teaspoon chopped coriander
½ teaspoon chopped chilli
salt and freshly ground black pepper

Nutritional breakdown
(per portion)

Protein 2.6 g
Fat 5.5 g
Sugar 64.0 g
Carbohydrate 64.9 g
Energy 308 k cal

1 In a bowl, mix together the **sweetcorn and peas**.
2 In a separate bowl, mix **all the other ingredients**.
3 Combine the two separate bowls. Leave in the refrigerator for 30 minutes before serving.

ONION relish

Serves 4

1 large onion, chopped
1 large red onion, chopped
1 ½ teaspoons olive oil and garlic mix
  (see page 27)
¼ teaspoon salt
freshly ground black pepper
1 tablespoon brown sugar
4 tablespoons vinegar

Nutritional breakdown
(per portion)

Protein 1.6 g
Fat 1.0 g
Sugar 6.8 g
Carbohydrate 9.7 g
Energy 51 k cal

1 Cook the **onions** in a non-stick pan in the **oil and garlic,** mixing, until brown Then add the **brown sugar** and stir until dissolved..
2 Season to taste, leave to cool and then add the **vinegar**. Store in a jar in the refrigerator.

GOURMET hip crisps

Serves 4

5 large potatoes
olive oil and chilli spray (see page 27)
sea salt and freshly ground black pepper

1 Preheat the oven to 200°C/Gas mark 6. Wash the potatoes thoroughly and slice thinly (about 1-2 mm). Spray with the **olive oil and chilli mix**. Sprinkle with **sea salt and pepper.**

2 Cook in the oven for 6 minutes, turn and cook for another 6 minutes. Cool and store in an airtight container.

BEET the treat gourmet crisps

Serves 4

5 large beetroot
oilve oil and thyme spray (see page 27)
sea salt and freshly ground black pepper

1 Preheat the oven to 200°C/Gas mark 6. Wash the **beetroot** thoroughly and slice thinly (about 1-2 mm). Spay minimally with the **oil** mix and sprinkle with **sea salt and pepper.**

2 Cook in the oven for 6 minutes on one side, turn over and cook for another 6 minutes. Cool and serve or store in airtight container.

RICE DISHES AND STIR-FRIES

Rice is a great carbohydrate and should be incorporated into your diet. Mix brown with white rice to ensure you get more nutrients and add colour to your cooking. When possible, try wild rice – it is exotic and tastes fantastic.

We recommend you serve rice with a range of the stir-fries in this chapter and the curries found on pages 84–9.

BRAZILIAN rice

Serves 6 to 8

3 onions, chopped
1 teaspoon vegetable oil
8 fresh tomatoes, chopped
1 teaspoon salt
100 g brown rice
750 ml water
1 mango, peeled and chopped

Nutritional breakdown
(per portion)

Protein 4.9 g
Fat 2.3 g
Sugar 6.0 g
Carbohydrate 56.8 g
Energy 253 k cal

1 In a covered saucepan, sauté the **onions** in the **oil** for 5 minutes on medium-high heat, stirring frequently.
2 Add the **tomatoes and salt** and continue to cook for 5 minutes.
3 Stir in the **rice and water**, cover and bring to the boil. Reduce the heat and simmer for about 40 minutes, until the rice is tender.
4 Just before serving, add the **chopped mango** and stir through.

Luscious advice

- **Brown rice** adds extra fibre, wild rice adds a touch of the exotic and you can always use just plain white rice.

ASIAN fried rice

Fried rice is fantastic but in many restaurants it is full of oil and fat. We've come up with a recipe that has flavour and kick.

Serves 6

3 medium onions, chopped
3 cloves garlic, finely chopped
3-4 tablespoons Thai curry paste
1 tablespoon vegetable oil
3 medium carrots, chopped
1 small Chinese cabbage, finely chopped
1 pepper, deseeded and chopped
500 g cooked wild and brown rice
5 tomatoes, chopped
200 g pineapple, chopped
6 tablespoons mung bean sprouts
3 tablespoons soy sauce
2 tablespoons chopped fresh mint
2 tablespoon chopped fresh coriander or basil

Nutritional breakdown
(per portion)

Protein 6.3 g
Fat 3.9 g
Sugar 12.0 g
Carbohydrate 42.3 g
Energy 219 k cal

1 In a large non-stick pan, sauté the **onions, garlic and curry paste** in the **oil** for about 5 minutes.
2 Add the **carrots and the cabbage** and cover and cook for 5 minutes, stirring occasionally. Then add the **peppers**, cover and cook for 3 to 4 minutes, until the **vegetables** are just tender.
3 Stir in the **rice, tomatoes, pineapple, sprouts and soy sauce** and cook, stirring constantly, until the **rice** is heated through.
4 Add the **mint and coriander or basil**, and if desired, **additional soy sauce** or **curry paste**.

RICE and chestnuts

Serves 4

3 tablespoons dried apricots, chopped into quarters
125 ml hot water
200 g jasmine rice, dry
5 tablespoons sliced water chestnuts
3 gherkins, cut into thin julienne strips
2 tablespoons fresh mint, chopped

DRESSING
2 tablespoons lemon juice
¼ teaspoon freshly ground black pepper

Nutritional breakdown
(per portion)

Protein 5.4 g
Fat 0.5 g
Sugar 8.0 g
Carbohydrate 49.5 g
Energy 224 k cal

1 Soak the **chopped apricots** in the hot water. Set aside for 30 minutes.
2 Cook the **jasmine rice** as on packet directions, drain and rinse and set aside.
3 To make the dressing, drain the **apricots** and place **2 tablespoons of the liquid** from the rice into a small bowl. Whisk in the **lemon juice and the pepper**. Pour over the rice.
4 Add the **apricots, water chestnuts and gherkins** to the rice and toss well. Just before serving, add the **fresh mint**.

RICE with lemongrass

Serves 4

200 g cooked jasmine rice
1 teaspoon vegetable oil
2 tablespoons finely chopped lemongrass
   or 2 teaspoons freshly grated lemon peel
4 cloves garlic
1 small fresh green chilli, finely chopped
   and with seeds removed for milder 'hot'
½ teaspoon salt
2 tablespoons chopped fresh basil

Nutritional breakdown
(per portion)

Protein 5.9 g
Fat 1.4 g
Sugar 0.6 g
Carbohydrate 43.3 g
Energy 212 k cal

1 Place the **rice** in a colander or sieve, rinse with cool water and set aside.
2 In a medium saucepan, preferably non-stick, warm the **oil** and add the **lemongrass or lemon peel, garlic, chilli and salt**. Cook on medium heat for 2 to 3 minutes, stirring frequently.
3 Add the **basil, rice and boiling water.** Cover and bring to the boil, reduce the heat and cook for 15 minutes. Remove from the heat and allow to sit for 5 minutes before serving.

BASIC vegetable risotto

Serves 4

750 ml low-fat vegetable stock
375 ml tomato juice
250 g sweetcorn
200 g Arborio rice
1 onion, chopped
3 tablespoons olive oil and water spray
  (see page 27)
8 tomatoes, chopped
2 courgettes, chopped
10 wild mushrooms, chopped
3 medium carrots, chopped

Nutritional breakdown
(per portion)

Protein 10.2 g
Fat 5.5 g
Sugar 15.4 g
Carbohydrate 57.4 g
Energy 318 k cal

1 Blend **500 ml of the stock** with the **tomato juice and sweetcorn** and set aside.
2 Heat the **oil** in a heavy non-stick pan and sauté the **onions**. Reduce to a low heat, add the **rice** and stir to stop the rice sticking and ensure that all the rice is covered with **oil and onions**.
3 Add the rest of the **stock**, stir and keep stirring until the stock is absorbed.
4 Add the **blended mixture, tomatoes, carrots, courgettes and mushrooms**. Keep stirring until the rice is tender. Cook on low for another 5 minutes.

VEGETABLE and chicken risotto

Serves 6

200 g lean chicken or turkey, cut into strips
2 peppers, deseeded and finely chopped
3 tablespoons roughly chopped basil
3 medium carrots, chopped
500 ml water
1 onion, chopped
1 tablespoon olive oil and water spray
  (see page 27)
25-30 wild mushrooms
2 courgettes, chopped
600 g peas
300 g Arborio rice
750 ml low-fat vegetable stock
freshly ground pepper, to taste

Nutritional breakdown
(per portion)

Protein 20.3 g
Fat 5.3 g
Sugar 6.6 g
Carbohydrate 56.8 g
Energy 354 k cal

1 Put the **chicken or turkey, pepper, basil and carrots** into a pan, cover with water and simmer until the chicken is cooked (5–10 minutes). Drain the water and set it to one side.
2 Heat the oil in a heavy non-stick pan and sauté the **onions, mushrooms, courgettes and peas**. Reduce to a low heat, add the **rice** and stir to stop the rice sticking and ensure that all the rice is covered with **oil and onions**.
3 Add **250 ml of the stock** and stir until it is absorbed. Add more **water** and stock and simmer for 15 minutes.
4 Add the **chicken or turkey, pepper, basil and carrots** and season to taste.
5 Remember, the risotto needs to absorb the water and stock, but ensure that there isn't too much.

BEETROOT risotto

Serves 4

5 beetroot, chopped
1 pepper, deseeded and roughly chopped
1 handful roughly chopped basil
3 medium carrots, chopped
500 ml water
3 tablespoons olive oil and water spray
  (see page 27)
1 onion, chopped
20 wild mushrooms
500 g Arborio rice
750 ml low-fat vegetable stock
300 g peas
salt and freshly ground pepper

Nutritional breakdown
(per portion)

Protein 20.2 g
Fat 6.6 g
Sugar 15.6 g
Carbohydrate 25.6 g
Energy 643 k cal

1 Put the **beetroot, pepper, basil and carrots** into a pan, cover with water and simmer until the **beetroot** is cooked (10–15 minutes). Drain the water and set it to one side.
2 Heat the **oil** in a heavy non-stick pan and sauté the **onions and mushrooms**. Reduce to a low heat, add the **rice** and stir to stop the rice sticking and ensure that all the rice is covered with **oil and onions**.
3 Add **250 ml of the stock** and stir until it is absorbed. Add some of the set aside water and more **stock** and simmer for 15 minutes.
4 Add the **peas** and simmer for a further 15 minutes. Season to taste

Luscious serving suggestions

• **Sprinkle** with fresh parsley.

• **Add** a small amount of freshly grated Parmesan cheese.

OVEN pumpkin risotto

Serves 4

2 litres low-fat chicken or vegetable stock
300 g Arborio rice
400 g chopped and cooked pumpkin
1 tablespoon grated lemon zest
¼ teaspoon ground nutmeg
6 tablespoons grated Parmesan cheese
Parmesan cheese curls, cut with
   a vegetable peeler (optional)
freshly grated nutmeg (optional)

Nutritional breakdown
(per portion)

Protein 15.2 g
Fat 9.3 g
Sugar 2.1 g
Carbohydrate 63.7 g
Energy 399 k cal

1 Preheat the oven to 200°C/Gas mark 6. In a shallow heavy-based pan, combine the **stock, rice, pumpkin, lemon peel and ground nutmeg**. Stir to mix well.
2 Bake in the oven until liquid begins to be absorbed (about 20 minutes). Stir again; then continue to bake, stirring often, until **rice** is tender to the bite and the mixture is creamy (about 25 more minutes). Stir in the **grated Parmesan cheese**.
3 To serve, transfer to a serving dish; garnish with **cheese curls**. If desired, sprinkle lightly with **freshly grated nutmeg**.

BASIC stir-fry

Serves 4

1 courgette, chopped
6 heads brocolli
1 carrot, chopped
100 g chopped green beans
500 g rice
1 tablespoon oil and water mix (see page 27)
1 small onion, chopped
10 mushrooms, chopped
1 red pepper, deseeded and chopped
1 green pepper, deseeded and chopped
½ teaspoon garlic powder
    or 1 garlic clove, crushed
1 teaspoon chilli
1 courgette, chopped
3 tablespoons light soy sauce
2 teaspoons parsley
1 handful chopped red cabbage
1 handful bean sprouts
4 tablespoons seasame seeds

> **Nutritional breakdown**
> (per portion)
>
> Protein 7.4 g
> Fat 6.8 g
> Sugar 7.1 g
> Carbohydrate 10.6 g
> Energy 127 k cal

1 Steam the **courgette, brocolli, carrots and green beans** in the microwave for 40 to 50 seconds. They should be crisp not mushy.
2 Cook the **rice**.
3 Heat the wok and sauté the **oil, onions, mushrooms and peppers**. Then add the **garlic, chilli and courgettes** and stir for another 2 minutes.
4 Add the **soy sauce, parsley, cabbage and sprouts** and stir for 1 minute. Add the **sesame seeds** and stir for another minute.
5 Serve with the **cooked rice**.

Luscious advice

- **The best way** to create a successful stir-fry is to chop everything before you start. This avoids making a big mess, and you can just stir everything into the pan so that it is a speedy event. This is the key to a great stir-fry: fast cooking and good preparation.

- **To re-heat rice** stored in a refrigerator, place rice in a ceramic bowl and cover with an upturned plate. Place in a microwave and heat for 1½ minutes. Gently remove from the microwave using gloves. You should invest in a food temperature gauge as the rice needs to be re-heated to 75°C to ensure it is fit for serving.

- **Stir-fry** is not an exact science, so remember, add or delete vegetables you like or don't like.

- **Gas is best** for cooking a stir-fry, and use a non-stick wok. Above all, have fun.

POLYNESIAN stir-fry

Serves 4

1 quantity basic stir-fry, but with coriander
    rather than parsley
200 g pineapple, drained and chopped
2 teaspoons fresh grated ginger

Nutritional breakdown
(per portion)

Protein 7.9 g
Fat 7.2 g
Sugar 12.5 g
Carbohydrate 16.1 g
Energy 153 k cal

1 Prepare the **ingredients** as above, adding the **pineapple and ginger**.
2 Cook as described above.

MANGO and orange mania

Serves 4

1 quantity basic stir-fry, but with coriander
  rather than parsley
1 fresh mango, peeled and chopped
2 oranges, peeled and chopped

Nutritional breakdown
(per portion)

Protein 8.5 g
Fat 7.1 g
Sugar 14.2 g
Carbohydrate 19.0 g
Energy 179 k cal

1 Prepare the **ingredients** as above, adding the **mango and orange**.
2 Cook as described above.

APPRECIATE the peach

Serves 4

1 quantity basic stir-fry, but without parsley
4 chopped apricots or peaches
1 teaspoon freshly grated ginger

Nutritional breakdown
(per portion)

Protein 8.1 g
Fat 7.1 g
Sugar 11.2 g
Carbohydrate 14.7 g
Energy 148 k cal

1 Prepare the **ingredients** as above, adding the **apricot or peach and ginger.**
2 Cook as described above.

MEAT of the matter

Serves 4

1 quantity basic stir-fry
300 g chopped lean chicken
  or 300 g lean beef, grilled

Nutritional breakdown
(per portion)

Protein 22.4 g
Fat 7.9 g
Sugar 5.6 g
Carbohydrate 8.2 g
Energy 189 k cal

1 Prepare the **ingredients** as above, adding the **chicken or beef**.
2 Cook as described above.

VEGETARIAN meat options

Serves 6

1 quantity basic stir-fry
200 g soya-based meat alternative
juice of 1 lemon
salt and freshly ground black pepper
basil
OR
1 quantity basic stir-fry
200 g chopped vegetarian chicken or ham

Nutritional breakdown
(per portion)

Protein 5.2 g
Fat 6.1 g
Sugar 4.2 g
Carbohydrate 7.1 g
Energy 99 k cal

1 Prepare the **ingredients** as above, adding the **vegetarian option** of your choice. If you are using the **soya-based meat alternative**, soak the **soya** in a mixture of the **lemon, salt, pepper and basil** for about an hour in the refrigerator in a dish covered in plastic wrap.
2 Cook as described above.

Luscious advice

- **To avoid using extra soy sauce or oil** if the mixture gets a bit dry, have some low-fat vegetable stock on standby and use a few tablespoons of that. It's great tasting and fat-free.

- **Vegetables** you may have not considered for stir-fries include:
    Chopped pumpkin
    Chopped potato
    Chopped Brussels sprouts
    Chopped spinach
    Red beans
    Chickpeas
    A range of nuts

LOW-FAT mee goreng

Serves 6

500 g hokkien noodles
oil and water mix (see page 27)
200 g tofu or 200 g lean chicken, thinly sliced
1 onion, finely chopped
1 medium tomato, finely chopped
2 tablespoons roughly chopped chives/spring onion
1 sprig curry leaves, finely chopped
2 tablespoons tomato sauce
1 tablespoon chilli sauce
2 teaspoons light soy sauce
1 egg, beaten
2 egg whites, beaten
1 microwaved potato, cut into small squares
1 fresh green chilli, sliced
pining for me salsa, to serve
 (see page 63)

> **Nutritional breakdown**
> (per portion)
>
> Protein 8.1 g
> Fat 3.3 g
> Sugar 2.5 g
> Carbohydrate 15.6 g
> Energy 120 k cal

1 Rinse the **noodles** in warm water, drain and set aside. Heat a large wok or deep frying pan and spray with **oil and water mix** before cooking the **tofu or chicken** until it is golden brown. Set aside.

2 Re-spray the wok and add the **onion**, cooking for 2 to 3 minutes or until soft, then add the **noodles, tomato, chives, curry leaves and sauces**. Cook over a low heat, stirring continuously for 3 to 4 minutes

3 Pour over the **beaten egg** and thickly **beaten egg whites** and leave to set for 45 seconds before stirring to combine. Add the **potato and tofu** before cooking for a further 30 seconds.

4 To serve, place onto a large serving dish. Garnish with the **green chilli** and serve with the **pining for me salsa**.

CURRIES

Let's face it, a curry down at the local Indian has started moving with the times. Indian has gone gourmet, and Indian curries are now the favourite British dish. A curry is great dinner party offering and, in our case, it's low-fat. Also, the fantastic thing about low-fat Indian cooking is you don't have to be too precise. If you want more of a certain vegetable or meat then add it.

BASIC vegetable curry

Serves 4

2 tablespoons curry paste
2 tablespoons olive oil and water spray (see page 27)
3 celery sticks, chopped
2 large red onions, chopped
3 garlic cloves, crushed
4 large potatoes, peeled and chopped
1 x 400 g can chopped tomatoes, including juices
2 large carrots, chopped
100 g peas
4 courgettes, chopped
200 g pumpkin
½ small brocolli, chopped
½ small cauliflower, chopped
3 handfuls chopped fresh spinach leaves or bok choy
5 tablespoons water

SPICES
6 cloves
½ teaspoon turmeric
1 teaspoon chilli powder (add more
  for extra kick)
5 cardomons
2 tablespoons chopped fresh coriander
salt and freshly ground black pepper

Nutritional breakdown
(per portion)

Protein 12 g
Fat 5.1 g
Sugar 10 g
Carbohydrate 29.4 g
Energy 177 k cal

1 Heat the **oil** in large non-stick pan and sauté the **curry paste, celery and onion**. Add the **garlic cloves** and stir for 3 minutes to let out flavour. Mix in the **spices**.

2 Add the **potatoes**, stir for 2 minutes and then add the remaining **vegetables, water and spices**. Cook on a low heat until tender. You may require more **chopped canned tomatoes**.

3 Serve with **steamed rice** and a fresh sprinkling of **coriander**.

4 If the curry is a little dry, add more **canned tomatoes** or **vegetable stock**.

Luscious advice

- **For a low-fat, creamy vegetable curry option** use coconut milk. You can get low-fat coconut cream in cans from most supermarkets or you can make it by steeping 5 tablespoons of desiccated coconut in 250 ml of skimmed milk overnight. Drain the desiccated coconut and discard. Mix in 125 ml of low-fat yoghurt or quark to the milk and you'll have an extremely low-fat coconut mixture.

- **To turn your vegetable curry into a low-fat coconut curry,** instead of one can of chopped tomatoes add only half a can. Replace the water with 250 ml of low-fat coconut cream or mock coconut cream mixture.

- **A vegetable curry can be made crunchy** by the addition of nuts. We recommend adding 4–5 tablespoons of almonds. This increases the fat content but it offers a good protein addition.

PEA and pumpkin or sweet potato curry

Serves 4

3 teaspoons cumin seeds
2 teaspoons coriander seeds
3 garlic cloves
1 teaspoon chilli
oil and water spray (see page 27)
2 medium red onions, finely chopped
500 ml low-fat vegetable stock
1 kg chunky pumpkin or sweet potatoes
400 g peas
250 ml whipped low-fat evaporated milk
250 ml low-fat coconut milk or skimmed milk
   and 1 teaspoon coconut essence

Nutritional breakdown
(per portion)

Protein 12.1 g
Fat 6.6 g
Sugar 13.4 g
Carbohydrate 23.0 g
Energy 177 k cal

1 Crush the **cumin and coriander seeds** with the **garlic and chilli**.
2 Heat a non-stick pan and brown the **onions** in a little **oil and water spray** and add the **ground spices**. Sauté for 2 minutes.
3 Add the **vegetable stock and pumpkin or sweet potato**. Bring to the boil then reduce the heat and simmer until the **vegetables** are just starting to turn soft (5–10 minutes).
4 Add the **peas, whipped evaporated milk, and milk and coconut essence** and simmer for a further 10 minutes.
5 Serve with **rice or couscous**. You can add sultanas for some additional flavour.

Luscious variations

• **Add chickpeas** for extra Moroccan influence and fibre.

• **Instead of pumpkin,** add carrot for an unusual curry.

FRUITY chicken curry

Serves 4

5 chicken breasts, skinned and chopped
1 tablespoon olive oil
1 onion, chopped
1 teaspoon ground cumin
2 teaspoons curry powder
2 large apples, sliced with skin on
8 tablespoons sultanas
1 banana
2 tablespoons honey
2 tablespoons freshly squeezed lemon juice
2 tablespoons water
½ can chopped tomatoes
250 ml low-fat coconut cream or evaporated
skimmed milk and ½ teaspoon coconut
essence
handful chopped coriander, to serve

> **Nutritional breakdown**
> (per portion)
>
> Protein 32.1 g
> Fat 6.5 g
> Sugar 68.4 g
> Carbohydrate 69.6 g
> Energy 447 k cal

1 Put the **chicken breast** into a microwavable container, cover with water and a lid and poach until the pinkness disappears. This is a great way to cook **chicken without fat**. We recommend poaching on high for 4 minutes. Drain, chop and set aside.
2 Place the **olive oil** into a large non-stick pan, sauté the **onions** and then add the **spices** and mix to release the flavours.
3 Add the **apples, sultanas, banana, honey, lemon and water**. Bring to the boil, then reduce the heat and simmer for 3 minutes. Add the **tomatoes, coconut cream or milk, and chicken** and simmer for a further 40 minutes.
4 Serve with **rice** and a **sprinkling of coriander**.

TANDOORI chicken

Serves 4

300 ml natural low-fat yogurt, drained (you may need extra)
10 cm ginger, finely chopped
1 large garlic clove, chopped
2 tablespoons paprika
4 teaspoons salt
3 cloves cinnamon
juice of 2 lemons
1 kg lean chicken, skinned
1 bay leaf
1 lemon, red onion and chilli pepper, to serve

Nutritional breakdown
(per portion)

Protein 86.5 g
Fat 8.8 g
Sugar 6.3 g
Carbohydrate 11.4 g
Energy 452 k cal

1 Mix all the **ingredients** except for the **chicken and bay leaf** in a food processor.
2 Marinate the **chicken** in the mixture with an **added bay leaf** overnight in the refrigerator.
3 Heat the oven to 180°C/Gas mark 4 and prepare an ovenproof dish by lining it with foil greased with **oil** . Place the **chicken** in the dish, fold over the foil and bake for 15 minutes. Turn the **chicken** over, return to the oven and bake for a further 15 minutes.
4 To serve, garnish the **chicken** with **lemon wedges, red onion slices and pieces of green chilli pepper**. Serve with **rice, naan, pitta bread or couscous**. This recipe comes courtesy of my friend Gita Amar.

PUMPKIN curry

Serves 4

500 g sweet pumpkin
5 tablespoons water
1 teaspoon olive oil
3 small red onions
2 teaspoons grated ginger
1 garlic clove
1 teaspoon cumin
1 teaspoon curry powder
1 teaspoon chopped chilli
4 tablespoons sultanas
200 ml vegetable stock (you may need more)
3 handfuls roughly ripped spinach
8 tablespoons roughly chopped coriander
  leaves
2 tablespoons almonds or walnuts

Nutritional breakdown
(per portion)

Protein 32.1 g
Fat 6.5 g
Sugar 68.4 g
Carbohydrate 69.6 g
Energy 447 k cal

1 Chop the **pumpkin** into large cubes and place in a microwave with the water. Cover and cook on high for 7 minutes. Set aside.
2 Heat the **oil** in a large non-stick pan and sauté the **onions**. Add the **spices and sultanas** to release the flavours. Then add the **stock** and bring to the boil. Reduce the heat and simmer for 5 minutes.
3 Add the **pumpkin** and cook for 5 minutes or until soft. Add the **spinach and coriander** and cook for a further 5 minutes.
4 Finally, add the **almonds or walnuts** and serve.

SATAYS AND KEBABS

Satay and kebabs are great as a meal with rice, as a snack or as party munchies. They also allow you to play around with tastes and make great barbecue food. When using satay sticks or bamboo skewers soak them in water for an hour before use to stop them scorching.

After the kebab recipes below, we give you some dipping sauces to accompany them. The great thing about low-fat cooking is that you can mix and match. Serve our kebabs with some of our rice dishes (see pages 72-5), add fruits and vegetables and different meats for flavour and serve with a selection of dipping sauces.

BASIC chicken kebabs

Serves 4

BASIC MARINADE
8 tablespoons soy sauce
2 tablespoons rice wine vinegar
2 tablespoons sugar
6 tablespoons chopped coriander
4 tablespoons chopped chives
1 teaspoon finely chopped chilli

500 g lean chicken breast, cut into
  2.5-cm cubes

Nutritional breakdown
(per portion)

Protein 27.6 g
Fat 3.8 g
Sugar 8.5 g
Carbohydrate 10.7 g
Energy 184 k cal

1 Mix together all the **marinade ingredients**.
2 Place the **chopped chicken** in a bowl and cover with the marinade mixture. Cover with plastic wrap and leave to marinate for at least 4 hours in the refrigerator.
3 Thread the **chicken** onto skewers and, using any leftover marinade, baste the kebabs with a brush and then grill or barbecue.
4 Serve with **rice or a side salad** and a **low-fat peanut sauce**.

VEGETABLE kebabs

Serves 4

MARINADE
250 ml soy sauce
2 tablespoons sugar
2 tablespoons rice wine vinegar
6 tablespoons chopped coriander
6 tablespoons chopped chives
1 teaspoon finely chopped chilli
5 tablespoons juice of your chosen fruit, e.g. lime

3 medium size carrots, cut into 2-cm wide slices
3 courgettes, cut into 2-cm wide slices
2 red peppers, cut into 2.5-cm squares
2 green peppers, cut into 2.5-cm squares
1 large sweet potato, steamed until crunchy
  and cut into 2.5-cm cubes
2 large beetroot, steamed until crunchy
  and cut into 2.5-cm cubes
2 celery sticks, cut into 2-cm slices
8 peaches or apricots, chopped,
  or 1 pineapple, chopped

Nutritional breakdown
(per portion)

Protein 11.5 g
Fat 1.5 g
Sugar 33.5 g
Carbohydrate 41.6 g
Energy 214 k cal

1 Mix together all the **marinade ingredients.**
2 Place the **vegetables** in a bowl and cover with the marinade mixture. Cover with plastic wrap and leave to marinate for at least 2 hours in the refrigerator.
3 Thread the **vegetable pieces** onto skewers – the order is up to you. Using any leftover marinade, baste the kebabs with a brush and then grill or barbecue.

BEEF kebabs

Serves 6

MARINADE
125 ml soy sauce
2 tablespoon sesame oil
1 handful finely chopped chives
1 garlic clove, grated
2 tablespoon brown or demerara sugar
1 teaspoon grated fresh ginger
1 teaspoon chilli powder
125 ml water

500 g lean steak, cut into 2.5-cm cubes

Nutritional breakdown
(per portion)

Protein 17.8 g
Fat 6.2 g
Sugar 5.3 g
Carbohydrate 7.8 g
Energy 153 k cal

1 Mix together all the **marinade ingredients**.
2 Place the **chopped steak** in a bowl and cover with the mixture. Cover with plastic wrap and leave to marinate for at least 4 hours in the refrigerator.
3 Thread the **meat pieces** onto skewers. Using any leftover marinade baste the kebabs with a brush, and then grill or barbecue.

Luscious variations

- **The ginger adds extra kick,** so serving this with a sweet-tasting Asian sauce is a pleasant surprise.

- **Make a sauce for serving** using 125 ml lemon juice and 125 ml water mixed with 1 teaspoon of ginger – easy and deliciously tangy.

FISH kebabs

Serves 4

MARINADE
2 teaspoons finely chopped garlic
1 teaspoon chopped red or green chilli
3 teaspoons grated ginger
juice of 1 or 2 limes, dependent on size
125 ml pineapple juice
125 ml soy sauce
salt and freshly ground black pepper

1 kg monkfish, cut into 2.5-cm cubes
1 ripe mango, peeled and cut into
   2.5-cm cubes
2 bananas, cut into 2.5-cm slices

Nutritional breakdown
(per portion)

Protein 43.2 g
Fat 1.3 g
Sugar 17.1 g
Carbohydrate 21.4 g
Energy 263 k cal

1 Mix together all the marinade ingredients.
2 Place the **chopped fish** in a bowl and cover with the mixture. Cover with plastic wrap and leave to marinate for at least 2 hours in the refrigerator.
3 Thread the **fish, mango and banana pieces** onto skewers and using any leftover marinade baste the kebabs with a brush. Grill or barbecue.

For each of these dipping sauces, put all the ingredients into a food processor and blend until smooth. If there is sugar in the ingredients ensure it is dissolved.

BASIC dipping sauce

Serves 4

125 ml soy sauce
125 ml white wine vinegar
2 tablespoons brown sugar
2 teaspoon grated fresh garlic
2 teaspoons grated fresh ginger

Nutritional breakdown
(per portion)

Protein 3.1 g
Fat 0.1 g
Sugar 4.1 g
Carbohydrate 7.2 g
Energy 39 k cal

TOMATO-BASED dipping sauce

Serves 4

3 red onions, chopped
500 g vine-ripened tomatoes, chopped
1 tablespoon crushed garlic
2 red onions, chopped
125 ml red wine
1 handful chopped red or green basil leaves
4 tablespoons chopped fresh parsley
2 teaspoons salt
freshly ground black pepper
1 teaspoon chilli
2 teaspoons sugar

Nutritional breakdown
(per portion)

Protein 3.9 g
Fat 1.1 g
Sugar 9.3 g
Carbohydrate 13.6 g
Energy 97 k cal

DILLY Billy yoghurt

Serves 4

350 ml low-fat plain yoghurt,
4 tablespoons chopped fresh dill
2 tablespoons lime juice
1 teaspoon grated lime
½ teaspoon crushed garlic
salt and freshly ground black pepper

Nutritional breakdown
(per portion)

Protein 7.1 g
Fat 1.1 g
Sugar 9.6 g
Carbohydrate 9.8 g
Energy 75 k cal

FAKE me out teryaki sauce

Serves 4

250 ml soy sauce
3 tablespoons dry sherry
1 tablespoon garlic powder
1 teaspoon grated ginger
3 tablespoons brown sugar

Nutritional breakdown
(per portion)

Protein 7.6 g
Fat 0.1 g
Sugar 12.0 g
Carbohydrate 21.6 g
Energy 118 k cal

THAI me-up dipping sauce

Serves 4

2 tablespoons chopped mint leaves
250 ml low-fat milk
6 cloves garlic, crushed
3 tablespoons finely chopped lemongrass
2 tablespoons honey
2 teaspoons fish sauce
3 teaspoons soy sauce
1 teaspoon finely chopped chilli
½ teaspoon imitation coconut extract

Nutritional breakdown
(per portion)

Protein 4.6 g
Fat 1.2 g
Sugar 11.2 g
Carbohydrate 16.5 g
Energy 91 k cal

SWEET and sour dipping sauce

Serves 4

4 tablespoons white wine vinegar
1 teaspoon vegetable oil
200 ml unsweetened pineapple juice
2 tablespoons tomato ketchup
3 tablespoons brown sugar
salt

Nutritional breakdown
(per portion)

Protein 0.4 g
Fat 0.8 g
Sugar 18.5 g
Carbohydrate 18.6 g
Energy 77 k cal

PIZZAS

Pizzas are great fun foods but they can be laden with fat. So here we have come up with some low-fat bases and a fresh low-fat tomato purée. From these bases and the tomato purée you can build up the pizza of your dreams.

BASIC flour dough

Serves 2

1 tablespoon baking yeast
1 teaspoon sugar
250 ml very warm water
75 g rolled oats
100 g wholemeal bread flour
1 teaspoon olive oil
1 teaspoon salt
300 g unbleached white bread flour

Nutritional breakdown
(per portion)

Protein 26.2 g
Fat 6.5 g
Sugar 6.7 g
Carbohydrate 160.1 g
Energy 764 k cal

1 Preheat the oven to 200°C/Gas mark 6.

2 Combine the **yeast with the sugar and warm water** in a large mixing bowl and set aside until bubbles rise to the surface, about 5 minutes.

3 Whirl the **oats** in a food processor until they are the consistency of coarse flour.

4 When the **yeast** is thoroughly dissolved and frothy, about 7 to 10 minutes, add the **oat flour, wholemeal flour, oil, salt and enough of the white flour** to make a stiff dough. Turn out onto a lightly floured surface and knead for 5 to 7 minutes, until smooth and elastic, adding the **remaining flour** as needed.

5 Lightly **oil or spray** a large bowl. Place the dough in it, turn it once to coat, cover it with a damp towel, and allow to rise in a warm spot for about 30 minutes, or until doubled in size.

6 Then take out again, knead and roll out to the size you want – big pizza or small individual sizes.

7 Part cook the base for 2-3 minutes, then add **toppings** and cook again.

POTATO pizza dough

Makes 2 large pizzas

8 medium potatoes, roughly chopped
1 teaspoon chopped chives
1 teaspoon finely chopped thyme
125 ml skimmed milk
120 g flour

Nutritional breakdown
(per portion)

Protein 14.6 g
Fat 2.1 g
Sugar 9.3 g
Carbohydrate 114.6 g
Energy 508 k cal

1 Preheat the oven to 200°C/Gas mark 6.
2 Boil the **potatoes** and mash through with the **herbs and milk**. Slowly add the **flour** until you achieved a dough-like consistency. If it is still watery add some **more flou**r.
3 Roll the dough out onto a floured baking sheet. Cut a circular pizza base.
4 Put in the oven and bake for 15 minutes.
5 Take out and add the **topping** of your choice.

Luscious advice

• **Use any kind of herb** – try basil, coriander, and mixed herbs in your base.

• **You can also make this dough base** using sweet potato or pumpkin.

LUSCIOUS tomato topping

Serves 4

10 tomatoes, chopped
10 rehydrated sun-dried tomatoes
1 onion, finely chopped
1 large garlic clove, finely chopped
3 tablespoons chopped fresh basil
salt and freshly ground black pepper

Nutritional breakdown
(per portion)

Protein 4.0 g
Fat 1.3 g
Sugar 13.2 g
Carbohydrate 15.8 g
Energy 86 k cal

1 Place **all the ingredients** in food processor and blend to a purée for
2-3 minutes.
2 Store in a plastic container in the refrigerator. You can also freeze the mixture for
later use.

Luscious advice

• **Use** vine-ripened tomatoes.

• **For a thicker paste** use a greater portion of sun-dried tomatoes to
fresh tomatoes.

TOMATO, pineapple, ham and baby spinach pizza

Makes 1 pizza to serve 2 people

1 quantity of the base of your choice
spray oil (see page 27)
5 tablespoons luscious tomato topping
  (see opposite)
5 rehydrated sun-dried tomatoes, chopped
200 g fresh pineapple pieces, chopped
4 slices low-fat ham, chopped
4 tablespoons chopped basil
4 handfuls baby spinach, chopped
100 g low-fat cheese

Nutritional breakdown
(per portion)

Protein 38.6 g
Fat 5.6 g
Sugar 28.0 g
Carbohydrate 134.4 g
Energy 709 k cal

1 Preheat the oven to 200°C/Gas mark 6.
2 Take your prepared base and lay it on a lightly oiled baking sheet. Cover the base with the **luscious tomato topping** and sprinkle on the **rest of the ingredient**s, except for the **spinach and cheese**.
3 Meanwhile, steam the **spinach** in the microwave and add to the pizza. Finish with the **cheese**.
4 Place the pizza in the oven and cook until the **cheese** has melted and slightly browned, 5 to 10 minutes.

BABY spinach, mushroom, onion and cheese pizza

Serves 3

1 quantity of the base of your choice
spray oil (see page 27)
5 tablespoons luscious tomato topping
  (see page 98)
15 mixed mushrooms, chopped
200 g sautéed and chopped baby spinach
1 onion, finely chopped
1 teaspoon cayenne pepper
4 tablespoons grated low-fat cheese

Nutritional breakdown
(per portion)

Protein 17.9 g
Fat 4.7 g
Sugar 8.6 g
Carbohydrate 79.8 g
Energy 412 k cal

1 Preheat the oven to 200°C/Gas mark 6.
2 Take your **prepared base** and lay it on a lightly oiled baking sheet. Cover the base with the **Luscious tomato topping** and sprinkle on the rest of the ingredients, finishing with the **cayenne pepper and cheese**.
3 Place the pizza in the oven and cook until the **cheese** has melted and slightly browned, 5 to 10 minutes.

TURKEY, cranberry and mushroom pizza

Serves 3-4

1 quantity of the base of your choice
spray oil (see page 27)
5 tablespoons luscious tomato topping
  (see page 98)
150 g lean chopped turkey
½ cup cranberry chutney
  or cranberry jelly
7 mixed mushrooms, chopped
1 teaspoon chopped oregano

Nutritional breakdown
(per portion)

Protein 34.2 g
Fat 4.8 g
Sugar 33.0 g
Carbohydrate 103.2 g
Energy 566 k cal

salt and freshly ground black pepper
4 tablespoons grated low-fat cheese

1 Preheat the oven to 200°C/Gas mark 6.
2 Take your prepared base and lay it on a lightly oiled baking sheet. Cover the base with the **luscious tomato topping** and sprinkle on the **rest of the ingredients**, finishing with the **cheese**.
3 Place the pizza in the oven and cook until the **cheese** has melted and slightly browned, 5 to 10 minutes.

TUNA, chilli and sun-dried tomato pizza

Serves 4

1 quantity of the base of your choice
spray oil (see page 27)
5 tablespoons luscious tomato topping
  (see page 98
1 teaspoon chopped chilli
1 x 400 g can tuna flakes in brine, drained
3 teaspoons chopped basil
1 small red onion, chopped
1 onion, sliced
8 rehydrated sun-dried tomatoes, chopped
4 tablespoons grated low-fat cheese

Nutritional breakdown
(per portion)

Protein 29.8 g
Fat 3.4 g
Sugar 7.7 g
Carbohydrate 60.8 g
Energy 377 k cal

1 Preheat the oven to 200°C/Gas mark 6.
2 Take your prepared base and lay it on a lightly oiled baking sheet. Cover the base with the **luscious tomato topping**.
3 Mix the **chilli** through with the **tuna and basil** and sprinkle over the base. Then add the **remaining ingredients**, finishing with the **cheese**.
4 Place the pizza in the oven and cook until the **cheese** has melted and slightly browned, 5 to 10 minutes.

MIXED vegetable pizza

Serves 2

1 quantity of the base of your choice
spray oil (see page 27)
5 tablespoons luscious tomato topping (see page 98)
2 handfuls baby spinach, chopped and steamed
3 tomatoes, chopped
1 coloured pepper, chopped
1 courgette, chopped
10 mushrooms, chopped
1 onion, chopped
2 teaspoons basil, finely chopped
2 teaspoons parsley, finely chopped
2 teaspoons freshly ground black pepper
200 g sweetcorn, drained
4 tablespoons grated low-fat cheese

Nutritional breakdown
(per portion)

Protein 29.4 g
Fat 8.1 g
Sugar 26.4 g
Carbohydrate 110.9 g
Energy 603 k cal

1 Preheat the oven to 200°C/Gas mark 6.
2 Take your **prepared base** and lay it on a lightly oiled baking sheet. Cover the base with the **luscious tomato topping** and sprinkle on the rest of the ingredients, finishing with the **sweetcorn and cheese**.
3 Place the pizza in the oven and cook until the **cheese** has melted and slightly browned, 5 to 10 minutes.

SALMON pizza

Serves 4

1 quantity of the base of your choice
spray oil (see page 27)
5 tablespoons luscious tomato topping
  (see page 98) or low-fat mayonnaise with
  2 tablespoons chopped red onion
4 slices smoked organic salmon, chopped

Nutritional breakdown
(per portion)

Protein 15.4 g
Fat 7.5 g
Sugar 6.6 g
Carbohydrate 59.6 g
Energy 352 k cal

2 teaspoons chopped dill
2 tablespoons drained capers
2 tablespoons chopped green olives in brine
40 g low-fat cheese of your choice

1 Preheat the oven to 200°C/Gas mark 6.
2 Take your prepared base and lay it on a lightly oiled baking sheet. Cover the base with the **luscious tomato topping** or the **mayo and onion combo** and sprinkle on the rest of the **ingredients**, finishing with the **cheese**.
3 Place the pizza in the oven and cook until the **cheese** has melted and slightly browned, 5 to 10 minutes.

BEETROOT, sweet potato and spinach pizza

Serves 4

1 quantity of the base of your choice
spray oil (see page 27)
1 small red onion, chopped
3 beetroot, steamed and mashed
2 sweet potatoes, steamed and chopped
2 teaspoons basil or coriander
1 tablespoon quark
3 handfuls baby spinach, steamed
  and chopped
100 g pumpkin
4 tablespoons grated low-fat cheese

Nutritional breakdown
(per portion)

Protein 30.7 g
Fat 6.7 g
Sugar 25.6 g
Carbohydrate 144.1 g
Energy 723 k cal

1 Preheat the oven to 200°C/Gas mark 6.
2 Take your **prepared base** and lay it on a lightly oiled baking sheet.
3 Mix the **red onion with the mashed beetroot** and spread over the base. Sprinkle with the **sweet potato and herbs**.
4 Mix together the **quark and chopped spinach, spread onto the base** and then sprinkle over it the **pumpkin** and finally the **grated cheese**.
3 Place the pizza in the oven and cook until the **cheese** has melted and slightly browned, 5 to 10 minutes.

Pasta dishes

Pesto is a great pasta sauce and you can use it for a range of other foods as well. It's fantastic in a sandwich or with a canapé and is even useful for flavouring savoury muffins and cakes. The problem is that some pesto is high in fat because of the oil added in the production process. So here are some easy, lower in fat pesto sauces you will enjoy.

BASIC pesto sauce

Serves 6-8

200 ml low-fat vegetable stock
2 garlic cloves, crushed
12 tablespoons chopped basil leaves
2 tablespoons pine nuts
6 tablespoons grated low-fat Parmesan cheese

Nutritional breakdown
(per portion)

Protein 5.2 g
Fat 3.5 g
Sugar 0.3 g
Carbohydrate 3.5 g
Energy 66 k cal

1 Heat the **stock and crushed garlic** in a pan and leave to cool.
2 Put the **basil leaves** in a food processor. Then add the **pine nuts, stock and cheese** and blend for about 2 minutes.

Luscious advice

• **The less you blend,** the chunkier your sauce – some people like a thick sauce.

• **Cook 200 g pasta** – any type. Grill some lean chicken, cut into chunks and mix through with 2 tablespoons of pesto – hey presto! – pesto pasta chicken.

THREE-HERB pesto

Serves 6–8

300 ml low-fat vegetable stock (you may need
   more)
6 garlic cloves, crushed
250 g fresh basil leaves
8 tablespoons fresh parsley sprigs
4 tablespoons fresh oregano leaves
2 tablespoons pine nuts
8 tablespoons grated low-fat Parmesan cheese

Nutritional breakdown
(per portion)

Protein 8.6 g
Fat 4.9 g
Sugar 0.8 g
Carbohydrate 5.4 g
Energy 100 k cal

1 Heat the **stock and crushed garlic** in a pan and leave to cool.
2 Put all the **herbs** in a food processor. Then add the **pine nuts, stock and cheese** and blend for about 2 minutes.

OUR red pepper pesto

Serves 4

4 red peppers, deseeded and roughly chopped
10 tablespoons chopped basil leaves
3 tablespoons balsamic vinegar
pinch of ground cinnamon
sea salt and freshly ground black pepper
3 garlic cloves, crushed
125 ml low-fat vegetable stock
100 g pine nuts
1 teaspoon dry mustard
1 teaspoon fresh coriander

Nutritional breakdown
(per portion)

Protein 5.3 g
Fat 9.6 g
Sugar 4.0 g
Carbohydrate 9.0 g
Energy 140 k cal

1 Simply put all the **ingredients** in a food processor and blend until smooth.
2 Serve immediately.

SUN-DRIED tomato and basil pesto

Serves 4

12 tablespoons chopped basil leaves
12 rehydrated sun-dried tomatoes
4 tablespoons pine nuts
250 ml low-fat vegetable stock
salt and freshly ground black pepper
2 garlic cloves, crushed
4 tablespoons low-fat Parmesan cheese

Nutritional breakdown
(per portion)

Protein 7.4 g
Fat 6.4 g
Sugar 3.2 g
Carbohydrate 7.5 g
Energy 115 k cal

1 Simply put **all the ingredients** in a food processor
  and blend until smooth.
2 Serve immediately.

EVEN simpler tomato and basil pesto

Serves 8

250 g basil leaves
6 vine-ripened tomatoes, chopped
3 garlic cloves, crushed
4 tablespoons pine nuts
125 ml low-fat vegetable stock

Nutritional breakdown
(per portion)

Protein 6.3 g
Fat 6.7 g
Sugar 4.9 g
Carbohydrate 11.9 g
Energy 131 k cal

1 Simply put **all the ingredients** in a food
processor and blend until smooth.
2 Serve immediately.

Luscious variations

- **To add further colour** to your pesto use red rather than green basil. Red basil has an even stronger flavour too.

- **To spice up your pesto,** add some chilli to the mix.

Pesto suggestions

- **French stick pesto:** Cut a French stick into individual slices, smear each slice with some low-fat cream cheese, add a slice of tomato and a small dollop of pesto sauce. Place a basil leave on top for an easy canapé.

- **Vegetable and basil crudités:** This is a yummy variation on a normal dip. Cut some carrot sticks, celery sticks, broccoli pieces, cauliflower pieces and courgette sticks. Place a small bowl of pesto in the middle of a large dish and lay vegetables around the dip. Yum!

- **Sandwiches:** Use pesto as a replacement for butter on salad sandwiches and to add kick to ham or chicken sandwiches.

- **Omelettes:** Half a teaspoon of pesto mixed with 1 teaspoon of hot water and then whisked into an omelette mixture adds a whole new dimension to the taste.

- **Baking:** Add 1 teaspoon of pesto to savoury baking products for extra flavour. Add a teaspoon of pesto to our low-fat pastry (see page 134) and you'll be in for a real treat.

PUMPKIN sauce

Serves 4

250 g pumpkin, peeled and chopped
2 small red onions, chopped
500 ml vegetable stock
1 tablespoon tomato purée
125 ml quark
1 tablespoon chopped fresh parsley
salt and freshly ground black pepper

Nutritional breakdown
(per portion)

Protein 15.5 g
Fat 5.9 g
Sugar 0.9 g
Carbohydrate 3.2 g
Energy 128 k cal

1 Mix together all the **ingredients** except the **parsley and seasoning**, cover and bring to the boil. Reduce the heat and simmer until the **pumpkin** is soft, about 10-15 minutes.

2 Leave to cool and then transfer to a food processor. Add the **quark** and blend until smooth. **Season** to taste.

3 Reheat if you want, and serve with **pasta** or as a sauce for vegetables or meat, mixing in the **parsley** just before pouring over the meal.

Luscious variations

• **Add chilli** to the mix for extra zing.

• **Coriander** in the mix will give this a Thai flavour.

CARROT chilli sauce

Serves 4

6 medium carrots, peeled and chopped
½ small red onion
½ tablespoon tomato purée
250 ml vegetable stock
1 garlic clove
½ teaspoon chilli
1 tablespoon low-fat yoghurt or quark

Nutritional breakdown
(per portion)

Protein 1.5 g
Fat 0.7 g
Sugar 3.9 g
Carbohydrate 5.4 g
Energy 33 k cal

1 Put **all the ingredients** except for the **yoghurt or quark** in a non-stick pan, cover and bring to the boil. Reduce the heat and simmer until the **carrots** are soft, approximately 10 minutes.
2 Leave to cool and then transfer to a food processor. Add the **yoghurt or quark** and blend until smooth. **Season** to taste and serve.

ASPARAGUS cream-like pasta sauce

Serves 4

15 fresh asparagus sticks
500 ml vegetable stock
1 small onion, chopped
1 garlic clove, crushed
250 ml low-fat yoghurt or quark
salt and freshly ground black pepper

Nutritional breakdown
(per portion)

Protein 2.7 g
Fat 1.2 g
Sugar 9.4 g
Carbohydrate 11.5 g
Energy 66 k cal

1 Chop the woody section from all the **asparagus sticks**. Put the **vegetable stock, onions and garlic** into a non-stick pan. Add **10 of the asparagus sticks**, cover and bring to the boil. Simmer until the **asparagus** is soft, about 5 minutes.
2 Leave to cool and transfer to a food processor. Add the **yoghurt or quark** and blend until smooth. Season to taste. Cut the **remaining asparagus** into 1-cm sections. Put **2 tablespoons of water** and the **asparagus** in a bowl and cover with plastic wrap. Cook on high for 2 minutes. Add to sauce and pour over **pasta.**

LOW-FAT tomato pasta sauce

Serves 4–6

2 red onions, chopped
3 garlic cloves, finely chopped
1 teaspoon olive oil
100 ml wine
8 medium sun-ripened tomatoes, chopped
10 olives
2 tablespoons balsamic vinegar
1 tablespoon sugar
1 tablespoon chopped fresh basil
2 tablespoons tomato purée
¼ teaspoon freshly ground black pepper
2 tablespoons chopped fresh parsley

Nutritional breakdown
(per portion)

Protein 4.3 g
Fat 4.1 g
Sugar 13.5 g
Carbohydrate 17.5 g
Energy 120 k cal

1 Heat a non-stick pan and sauté the **onions and garlic** in the **oil.** Add the **wine** and then the **tomatoes, olives** and the rest of the **ingredients** except for the **parsley**.
2 Reduce the heat to medium and cook, uncovered, for about 15 minutes. Stir in the **parsley**.

Luscious variations

• **Add sweetcorn,** beans, low-fat ham, low-fat chicken, sliced low-fat vegetarian sausage, mushrooms or other vegetables to create your own special tomato pasta sauce.

PASTA primavera

Serves 6

6 garlic cloves, finely chopped
2 teaspoons olive oil
3 x 400 g cans chopped tomatoes
100 ml dry white wine
5 tablespoons chopped fresh basil leaves
1 small red onion, thinly sliced
2 small carrots, peeled and cut into 5-cm pieces
450 g asparagus, cut into 5-cm pieces
1 red pepper, cut into 5-cm matchsticks
1 small courgette, cut into 5-cm matchsticks
100 g fresh or frozen green peas
salt and freshly ground black pepper
450 g fettuccini
4 tablespoons grated Pecorino
  or Parmesan cheese

Nutritional breakdown
(per portion)

Protein 8.9 g
Fat 4.0 g
Sugar 6.9 g
Carbohydrate 12.8 g
Energy 131 k cal

1 Bring to the boil a covered pan of water large enough to accommodate a colander or steamer basket.
2 Meanwhile heat a non-stick pan and sauté the **garlic** in the **oil** for about 2 minutes. Add the **tomatoes and wine**, cover and cook on medium heat for about 5 minutes. Add the **basil and red onions** and remove from the boil, leaving to simmer.
3 When the water in the other pan is boiling, blanch the **vegetables**. Put the **carrots** in first. After 1 minute, add the **asparagus and peppers**. After another minute, add the **courgettes and peas**. Cook for 1 minute more and then lift all of the **vegetables** from the colander and set aside to drain. Reserve the pot of boiling water for cooking the **pasta**. Stir the **vegetables** into the **tomato sauce**. Add **salt and pepper** to taste. Cover and set aside.
4 Cook the **pasta** according to the packet's instructions. Drain, reserving 4 tablespoons of the cooking water. Toss the **pasta** with the **reserved cooking water and 3 teaspoons of the grated cheese**. Top with the **tomato vegetable sauce**, sprinkle with the **remaining cheese** and serve immediately.

PASTA with aubergines

Serves 4 to 6

2 medium aubergines
salt
2 teaspoons olive oil
3 large garlic cloves, finely chopped
3 onions, chopped
3 x 400 g cans plum tomatoes, undrained
1 tablespoon dried basil
450 g ziti, penne or macaroni
2 tablespoons low-fat ricotta cheese

Nutritional breakdown
(per portion)

Protein 16.1 g
Fat 3.5 g
Sugar 12.1 g
Carbohydrate 83.1 g
Energy 407 k cal

1 Cut the **aubergines** lengthways or crossways into 2.5-cm thick slices. Lightly salt each slice, stack the slices, and then set them aside for about 20 minutes.
2 Preheat the oven to 240°C/Gas mark 9.
3 Heat the **oil** in a large pan and sauté the **garlic and onions** until the **onions** are golden. Stir often enough to prevent sticking. Chop the **tomatoes** and add to the saucepan. Add the **basil** and continue to cook, stirring occasionally, until the sauce begins to thicken.
4 While the **tomato sauce** cooks, rinse and dry the **aubergine slices**. Prepare a large baking sheet with **cooking spray or a light coating of vegetable oil**. Place a single layer of **aubergine slices** on the baking sheet and bake, uncovered, for 15 minutes. With a metal spatula, carefully flip the slices over and bake for another 15 minutes.
5 About 5 minutes before the **aubergine** finishes baking, bring a large covered pot of water to the boil.
6 When the **aubergine slices** are tender and browned, remove them from the oven, allow to cool slightly and then cut into 1.2 x 7.5-cm strips. Stir the **aubergine** into the **tomato sauce** and cook for about 10 more minutes.
7 When the water boils, stir in the **pasta**, and cook according to the packet's instructions. Drain and serve immediately, topped with the **tomato-aubergine sauce and grated cheese**.

LOW-FAT carbonara with asparagus

Serves 6

2 tablespoons grated fresh Parmesan cheese
4 tablespoons low-fat ricotta cheese
100 ml skimmed milk
1 egg
2 tablespoons chopped chives
¼ teaspoon salt
225 g bow tie pasta
spray oil (see page 27)
4 low-fat ham slices, chopped
2 garlic cloves, finely chopped
1 onion, chopped
18 pieces of asparagus, diagonally sliced
  and trimmed
1 handful chopped parsley
freshly ground black pepper

Nutritional breakdown
(per portion)

Protein 15.3 g
Fat 3.4 g
Sugar 5.0 g
Carbohydrate 34.7 g
Energy 221 k cal

1 In a small bowl, mix **the cheeses** with the **milk, egg, chives** and **salt** in a small bowl. Set aside.

2 Cook the **pasta** according to the packet's instructions. Drain and set aside.

3 Heat some **spray oil** in a large non-stick pan and cook the **ham and garlic** until crisp.

4 Steam the **asparagus** in the microwave until al dente. Stir into the **ham mixture**, add the **cheese, egg, chives and milk mixture** and stir for 30 seconds. Pour over the **pasta** and quickly mix through before serving. Add **parsley and pepper** to taste.

LOW-FAT lasagne

Serves 4

9 pieces lasagne
1 teaspoon vegetable oil and water spray (see page 27)
1 medium onion, chopped
2 garlic cloves, crushed
10 mushrooms, chopped
150 g chopped steamed pumpkin
3 carrots, chopped
2 medium courgettes
1 pepper, deseeded and chopped
4 tablespoons roughly chopped fresh parsley
500 ml low-fat tomato pasta sauce
200 g low-fat ricotta cheese
200 ml quark
8 tablespoons grated low-fat mozzarella cheese
2 tablespoons grated Parmesan cheese
300 g frozen spinach, thawed and
  thoroughly drained
freshly ground black pepper
¼ teaspoon salt
1 tablespoon chopped fresh basil
½ teaspoon dried oregano
  or 1 tablespoon chopped fresh oregano

Nutritional breakdown
(per portion)

Protein 26.0 g
Fat 11.9 g
Sugar 15.0 g
Carbohydrate 22.2 g
Energy 294 k cal

1 Cook the **pasta** according to the packet's instructions. Drain and cover with cool water until ready to use. Preheat the oven to 180°C/Gas mark 4.
2 Heat the **oil** in a non-stick pan and sauté the **onions, garlic and mushrooms**. Add the **pumpkin, carrots and courgettes** and sauté for 3 minutes. Then add the **pepper, parsley and tomato sauce** and simmer for 5 minutes.
3 In a separate bowl, mix the **ricotta, quark and half the grated cheeses and spinach** and add **pepper** to taste.
4 In a non-stick roasting pan lay out a layer of the **vegetable mixture** and a layer of the **pasta sheets**, then on top a layer of the **cheese and spinach mixture**, more **vegetables,** more **pasta** and so on. On the final layer of **pasta**, sprinkle the **remaining cheeses**. Cook in the oven for 40 minutes, until browned on top.

LOW-FAT chicken or turkey lasagne

Serves 4–6

9 pieces lasagne
1 tablespoon oil and water spray (see page 27)
1 onion, chopped
1 green pepper, chopped
3 courgettes, chopped
10 mushrooms, chopped
250 ml low-fat tomato pasta sauce
100 g low-fat Cheddar cheese, grated
250 ml quark
400 g low-fat cottage cheese
4 tablespoons Parmesan cheese
20 slices low-fat chicken or turkey, finely
  chopped
garlic powder

Nutritional breakdown
(per portion)

Protein 50.4 g
Fat 10.9 g
Sugar 12.5 g
Carbohydrate 16.8 g
Energy 363 k cal

1 Cook the **pasta** according to the packet's instructions. Drain and cover with cool water until ready to use.
2 Preheat the oven to 180°C/Gas mark 4.
3 Heat the oil in a non-stick pan and sauté all the **vegetables and meat**. Add the **low-fat tomato pasta sauce**.
4 Mix together all the **cheeses**, reserving half for the topping.
5 In an oven-proof dish, lay down a layer of the **turkey or meat** and add some **garlic powder**. Cover with **pasta sheets**, top with some of the **vegetable mixture**, top that with a layer of the **cheese mixture**. Add more **chicken** and then a layer of **pasta sheets** and so on until you finish with a layer of **pasta sheets**. Sprinkle the **remaining cheeses** over the top and cook in the oven for 30 to 40 minutes, until browned on top.

SWEET DELIGHTS

Yum, something sweet is always a welcome treat. These low-fat delights will please you and your friends.

If you have a sweet tooth, finding low-fat options can be difficult. So here we first have a few fruity spreads that we think you'll love. Use them on toast and on pancakes or as an alternative to cream when serving cake or pudding. Basically, they are scrummy. Then we move onto muffins, scones, biscuits, cakes and finally some truly scrumptious low-fat desserts.

Make each of the following spreads in exactly the same way. Heat a non-stick pan and add all the ingredients. Bring to the boil, then reduce the heat and simmer for 20 minutes. Cool and transfer to a food processor. Blend until smooth.

APRICOT spread

Serves 6–8

250 ml freshly squeezed orange juice
20 dried apricots, chopped
250 ml water
2 tablespoons sugar

Nutritional breakdown
(per portion)

Protein 2.3 g
Fat 0.3 g
Sugar 27.5 g
Carbohydrate 27.5 g
Energy 115 k cal

PEACH spread

Serves 6–8

250 ml freshly squeezed orange juice
20 dried peaches, chopped
250 ml water
2 tablespoons sugar

Nutritional breakdown
(per portion)

Protein 1.7 g
Fat 0.3 g
Sugar 31.6 g
Carbohydrate 31.6 g
Energy 128 k cal

APRICOTS, apple and sultanas

Serves 6–8

500 ml apple juice
20 dried apricots, chopped
20 dried apples slices, chopped
8 tablespoons sultanas
250 ml water
2 tablespoons sugar

Nutritional breakdown
(per portion)

Protein 3.2 g
Fat 0.6 g
Sugar 63.3 g
Carbohydrate 63.3 g
Energy 256 k cal

PRUNE spread

Serves 8

250 ml apple juice
20 dried prunes, chopped
250 ml water
2 tablespoons sugar

Nutritional breakdown
(per portion)

Protein 1.4 g
Fat 0.7 g
Sugar 31.3 g
Carbohydrate 31.3 g
Energy 129 k cal

Luscious advice

- **This is a great technique** because you can make a spread with whatever dried fruit you favour.

- **Serve the spreads** on a top quality fresh organic slice of bread with a layer of low-fat ricotta.

- **For a creamy variation,** mix 2 additional tablespoons of sugar and 200 g of quark and blend and serve immediately.

BLUEBERRY muffins

Serves 4

400 g self-raising flour
1½ tablespoons baking powder
6 tablespoons bran
3 tablespoons sugar or sugar sweetener
3 egg whites, whipped
250 ml apple puree
1 banana, mashed
375 ml skimmed milk
200 g blueberries

Nutritional breakdown
(per portion)

Protein 19.2 g
Fat 3.0 g
Sugar 60.8 g
Carbohydrate 142.7 g
Energy 638 k cal

1 Preheat the oven to 200°C/Gas mark 6.
2 In a bowl, mix together the **flour, baking powder, bran and sugar**.
3 In a separate bowl, whisk the **egg whites** until they form stiff peaks and mix in the **apple purée, mashed banana and milk**.
4 Stir in the **dry ingredients** and then gently fold in the **blueberries**.
5 Spray a non-stick muffin tray with **low-fat non-stick spray** and then dollop the mixture into each compartment. Bake in the oven for 17 minutes. Before removing, check that the muffins spring back when lightly pressed. You may need to bake them for an extra 2-3 minutes. Leave to cool on a wire rack.

Luscious advice

- **Depending on the consistency** of the purée and blueberries, you may have to add a little extra flour.

- **Purchase muffin tins** that allow you to make mini-muffins – these can then become mini-snacks and you can pop a few into a zip-lock bag for munching.

Luscious variations

Variety is the spice of life, so here are some novel ways to use the basic muffin mixture minus the blueberries.

- **Raspberry rushes:** replace half the blueberries with raspberries.

- **Apricot and walnuts:** replace the blueberries with 1 x 400 g can apricots, drained and chopped. Add 50 g finely chopped walnuts. For extra punch we recommend that you replace the milk with a 30 per cent nectar juice, 70 per cent milk mixture.

- **Banana and sultanas:** replace the blueberries with another 2 bananas mashed. Add 16 tablespoons of sultanas.

- **Mango me:** This is a nice tropical flavoured muffin. Replace the blueberries with 1 x 400 g canned or fresh mango, chopped. Instead of milk add 125 ml of syrup from the canned mango and 125 ml milk.

- **Dried fruit medley:** Replace the blueberries with 4 chopped apricots, 4 chopped dates, 4 chopped peaches, 4 chopped pears, 3 tablespoons sultanas and 4 chopped dried apple rings.

SAVOURY muffins

Serves 4

400 g plain flour
3 teaspoons baking powder
1 teaspoon salt
100 g cornmeal
1 teaspoon freshly ground black pepper
2 tablespoons wheatgerm
2 egg white, whipped
2 eggs
375 ml skimmed milk

Nutritional breakdown
(per muffin)

Protein 22.4 g
Fat 6.0 g
Sugar 7.7 g
Carbohydrate 106.5 g
Energy 550 k cal

1 Preheat the oven to 200°C/Gas mark 6.
2 In one bowl, mix together the **dry ingredients**.
3 In a separate bowl, mix together the **remaining ingredients**.
4 Combine the contents of both bowls.
5 Spray a non-stick muffin tray with low-fat spray and dollop the mixture into each compartment. Bake in the oven for 15 minutes and leave to cool on a wire rack.

HERB and cheese muffins

Serves 4

1 quantity of the basic savoury muffins recipe
4 tablespoons chopped chives
1 teaspoon dill
1 teaspoon chopped thyme
4 tablespoons grated low-fat cheese
3 tablespoons grated Parmesan cheese

Nutritional breakdown
(per muffin)

Protein 25.3 g
Fat 7.1 g
Sugar 6.6 g
Carbohydrate 89.3 g
Energy 506 k cal

1 Following the savoury muffins method, add all the **ingredients** to the dry mix bowl except for the **Parmesan cheese**.
2 When you put the mixture into the muffin tins sprinkle a little **Parmesan cheese** on top of each. Bake for 15 minutes.

For these variations, add the ingredients to the basic Savoury muffins ingredients and make as described opposite.

CHILLI corn and cheese muffins

Serves 4

1 quantity of the basic savoury muffins recipe
2 teaspoons chopped chilli
40 g grated Parmesan cheese
80 g grated low-fat Cheddar cheese
¼ teaspoon cayenne pepper
1 x 400 g can sweetcorn, drained

Nutritional breakdown
(per muffin)

Protein 27.8 g
Fat 8.4 g
Sugar 7.4 g
Carbohydrate 97.6 g
Energy 559 k cal

HAM and corn muffins

Serves 4

1 quantity of the basic savoury muffins recipe
5 slices low-fat ham, chopped
1 x 400 g can sweetcorn, drained
salt and freshly ground black pepper
40 g grated Parmesan cheese

Nutritional breakdown
(per muffin)

Protein 26.0 g
Fat 7.3 g
Sugar 7.5 g
Carbohydrate 97.5 g
Energy 542 k cal

THE basic biscuit recipe

Makes 15–20 biscuits

100 g low-fat margarine
150 g caster sugar
2 egg whites, beaten until peaked
125 ml oil and water mixture
350 g plain flour
2 teaspoons vanilla essence
1 egg yolk
⅛ teaspoon salt

Nutritional breakdown
(per biscuit)

Protein 2.6 g
Fat 3.0 g
Sugar 9.4 g
Carbohydrate 24.2 g
Energy 128 k cal

1 Preheat the oven to 180°C/Gas mark 4.
2 Cream together the **margarine and half the sugar**. Add the **beaten egg whites** and then the **water and oil mixture.** Gently combine the rest of the ingredients in the mixture until you end up with a dough-like consistency.
3 Roll out the dough and use a cutter to form the biscuits, or divide the dough into three sections and roll into logs. Place the logs on a dish, cover with plastic wrap and put into the refrigerator for 4 hours. Then cut the biscuits as you would cut bread. Transfer the dishes to a non-stick baking sheet greased with a little water and oil spray.
4 Cook the biscuits in the oven for about 15 minutes, until done.

CHOC attack

Makes 15-20 biscuits

1 quantity basic biscuit mixture
4 tablespoons low-fat cocoa powder

DECORATION
8 tablespoons icing sugar
2 tablespoons low-fat cocoa powder
3 tablespoons water
3 butterscotch sweets, crushed.

Nutritional breakdown
(per biscuit)

Protein 2.8 g
Fat 3.0 g
Sugar 16.9 g
Carbohydrate 31.8 g
Energy 158 k cal

1 Following the basic biscuit recipe opposite, add the **cocoa powder** when you add the **flour**.
2 When the biscuits are cooked, sift the **icing sugar and cocoa powder** into a bowl. Slowly add the **water**, mixing all the time, until you have a smooth thick consistency. Dip half of each biscuit into the **icing**. Place the biscuits on a wire rack and sprinkle the iced section with a little of the **crushed butterscotch sweets**.

CHOC orange attack

Makes 15–20 biscuits

1 quantity basic biscuit mixture
4 tablespoons low-fat cocoa powder
2 tablespoons orange juice

DECORATION
8 tablespoons icing sugar
2 tablespoons low-fat cocoa powder
3 tablespoons water
3 tablespoons finely shaved orange rind

Nutritional breakdown
(per biscuit)

Protein 2.9 g
Fat 3.0 g
Sugar 16.8 g
Carbohydrate 31.7 g
Energy 157 k cal

1 Following the basic biscuit recipe opposite, add the **cocoa powder** when you add the flour.
2 Add the **orange juice** at the same time as the water.
3 When the biscuits are cooked, sift the **icing sugar and cocoa powder** into a bowl. Slowly add the **water**, mixing all the time, until you have a smooth thick consistency. Dip half of each biscuit into the icing. Place the biscuits on a wire rack and sprinkle the iced section with a little of the **thinly sliced orange rind**.

LEMON is the essence

Makes 15–20 biscuits

1 quantity basic biscuit mixture
3 tablespoons fresh lemon juice
  or 1 teaspoon lemon essence

DECORATION
8 tablespoons icing sugar
2 teaspoons lemon essence
3 tablespoons water
thinly sliced lemon rind

Nutritional breakdown
(per biscuit)

Protein 2.7 g
Fat 3.0 g
Sugar 16.6 g
Carbohydrate 31.5 g
Energy 156 k cal

1 Following the basic biscuit recipe (page 122), add the **lemon juice or essence** at the same time as the **water**.
2 When the biscuits are cooked, sift the **icing sugar and cocoa powder** into a bowl. Slowly add the water, mixing all the time, until you have a smooth thick consistency. Dip half of each biscuit into the icing. Place the biscuits on a wire rack and sprinkle the iced section with a little of the **thinly sliced lemon rind**.

APRICOT surprise

Nutritional breakdown
(per biscuit)

Protein 2.7 g
Fat 3.0 g
Sugar 11.1 g
Carbohydrate 26.1 g
Energy 136 k cal

Makes 15–20 biscuits

1 quantity basic biscuit mixture
8 tablespoons apricot jam
2 tablespoons grated ginger

1 Follow the basic biscuit recipe (page 122) but just before baking, make a small indent in the middle of each biscuit and add about ⅓ tesapoon of **jam** and top with **a small piece of ginger**.
2 Bake as in the basic recipe.

ANGEL cake

Serves 12 slices

40 g cornflour
40 g plain flour
8 egg whites
225 g caster sugar, plus extra for sprinkling
1 teaspoon vanilla essence
90 ml orange-flavoured glacé icing (see below)
200 g icing sugar
3 tablespoons orange juice
a little icing sugar, to decorate

Nutritional breakdown
(per portion)

Protein 2.3 g
Fat 0.1 g
Sugar 22.6 g
Carbohydrate 28.2 g
Energy 115 k cal

1 Preheat the oven to 180°C/Gas mark 4.

2 Sift both the **flours** on to a sheet of greaseproof paper.

3 In a bowl, whisk the **egg whites** until very stiff and then gradually add the **sugar and vanilla essence**, whisking until the mixture is thick and glossy.

4 Gently fold in the **flour mixture** with a large metal spoon. Spoon into an ungreased 25-cm angel cake tin, smooth the surface and bake for about 45 to50 minutes, until the cake springs back when lightly pressed.

5 Sprinkle the piece of greaseproof paper with **caster suga**r and set an egg cup in the centre. Invert the cake tin over the paper, balancing it carefully on the egg cup. When cold, the cake will drop out of the tin.

6 To make the glacé icing, sift the **icing sugar** into a bowl and add the **orange juice**. Stir until smooth. You may need to add more orange juice.

7 Transfer the cake to a plate, spoon over the **glacé icing** and then dust with **icing sugar** and serve.

CARROT cake with lemon frosting

Serves 8

225 g wholemeal self-raising flour
2 teaspoons ground allspice
115 g light muscovado sugar
2 medium carrots, grated
50 g sultanas
50 ml sunflower oil
25 ml water
75 ml orange juice
75 ml skimmed milk
2 egg whites

FROSTING
350 g skimmed milk soft cheese
1 lemon rind, finely grated
60 ml clear honey
shreds of lemon rind, to decorate

Nutritional breakdown
(per portion)

Protein 11.0 g
Fat 5.9 g
Sugar 29.4 g
Carbohydrate 46.8 g
Energy 268 k cal

1 Preheat the oven to 180°C/Gas mark 4. Grease a deep 18-cm round cake tin and line the base with non-stick baking paper.
2 Sift the **flour and spice**, then sir in the **sugar, grated carrots and sultanas.**
3 Mix the **liquids**, then stir into the **dry ingredients**. Whisk the **egg whites** until stiff and then fold in evenly. Spoon into the tin and bake for 45 to 50 minutes.
4 Turn out and cool. For the frosting, beat together the **cheese, lemon rind and honey** until smooth. Spread over the top of the cooled cake, swirling with a palette knife. Decorate with **lemon rind**.

CRANBERRY and apple ring

Serves 8

125 g self-raising flour
1 teaspoon ground cinnamon
70 g light muscovado sugar
1 crisp eating apple, peeled, cored
  and chopped
70 g fresh or frozen cranberries
60 ml sunflower oil
150 ml apple juice
cranberry jelly and apple slices, to decorate

Nutritional breakdown
(per portion)

Protein 1.5 g
Fat 6.5 g
Sugar 15.4 g
Carbohydrate 27.0 g
Energy 164 k cal

1 Preheat the oven to 180°C/Gas mark 4. Lightly grease a 1-litre ring mould with oil.

2 Sift together the **flour and ground cinnamon**, then stir in the **sugar**.

3 Toss together the **chopped apple and cranberries**. Stir into the **dry ingredients**, then add the **oil and apple juice** and beat well.

4 Spoon the mixture into the prepared ring mould and bake for about 35 to 40 minutes, or until the cake is firm to the touch. Turn out the cake and leave to cool completely on a wire rack.

5 To serve, drizzle **warmed cranberry jelly** over the cake and decorate with **apple slices**.

LOW-FAT choc suprise

Serves 8

MARSHMALLOW CREAM
1 x 200 ml can skimmed evaporated milk
1 x 200 g packet of marshmallows

4 tablespoons low-fat cocoa
  or chocolate powder
130 g plain flour
pinch salt
1 teaspoon baking powder
6 egg whites, whipped
150 g caster sugar
1 tablespoon vanilla

Nutritional breakdown
(per portion)

Protein 6.5 g
Fat 0.3 g
Sugar 39.8 g
Carbohydrate 57.0 g
Energy 243 k cal

1 To make the marshmallow cream, whip the **evaporated milk** until peaked.
2 Melt the **marshmallows** in covered bowl in a microwave for 1 minute on high and mix into the **evaporated milk**.
3 Preheat oven at 170°C/Gas mark 3. Prepare a 20-cm square pan with cooking spray and flour.
4 To make the cake, in a mixing bowl combine the **cocoa powder, flour, salt, baking powder and baking soda**.
5 In another mixing bowl, combine the **egg whites, sugar, vanilla and marshmallow cream**. Mix
6 Mix together the **dry ingredients** with the **wet ingredients** just until moistened. Pour the mixture into prepared pan and bake for 30 minutes.

LOW-FAT carrot cake

Serves 8

300 g flour
1 pinch cloves
2 teaspoons baking powder
¼ teaspoon nutmeg
225 g caster sugar
1 x 400 g can crushed pineapple
2 tablespoons vegetable oil
1 teaspoon vanilla essence
8 carrots, grated
8 tablespoons sultanas
3 large egg whites

Nutritional breakdown
(per portion)

Protein 6.5 g
Fat 3.7 g
Sugar 60.7 g
Carbohydrate 90.1 g
Energy 396 k cal

1 Preheat the oven to 180°C/Gas mark 4. Line a 32 x 23-cm baking pan with foil. Coat with **vegetable oil cooking spray**.

2 In a bowl, combine the **flour, cloves, baking powder and nutmeg**..

3 In a separate bowl, beat the **sugar, pineapple, oil and vanilla essence** until smooth.

4 Beat in the **dry ingredients** until just combined. Then stir in the **carrots and sultanas**.

5 In a small bowl, beat the **egg whites** to stiff peaks. Fold into the **carrot mixture** in two batches with a rubber spatula. Pour the batter into the prepared pan.

6 Bake in the oven for 40 minutes or until a toothpick comes out cleanly. Cool in the pan on a wire rack. Invert the cake onto greaseproof paper and remove the pan and foil.

SPICED apple cake

Serves 8

250 g self-raising wholemeal flour
2 teaspoons baking powder
2 teaspoons ground cinnamon
350 g chopped dates
150 g light muscovado sugar
30 ml apple spread
240 ml apple juice
4 eggs, beaten
180 ml sunflower oil
4 eating apples, cored and grated
30 ml chopped walnuts

Nutritional breakdown
(per portion)

Protein 9.3 g
Fat 21.9 g
Sugar 55.5 g
Carbohydrate 75.3 g
Energy 513 k cal

1 Preheat the oven to 180°C/Gas mark 4. Grease and line a deep round 20-cm cake tin.

2 Sift the **flour, baking powder and cinnamon** into a mixing bowl, then mix in the **dates** and make a well in the centre.

3 Mix the **sugar with the apple spread** in a small bowl. Gradually stir in the **apple juice**. Add to the **dry ingredients with the eggs, oil and grated apples**. Mix thoroughly.

4 Spoon the mixture into the prepared cake tin, sprinkle liberally with **walnuts** and bake for 60 to 65 minutes or until a skewer inserted into the centre of the cake comes out cleanly. Transfer to a wire rack, remove the lining paper and leave to cool.

GINGER cake with fake cream

Serves 8

350 g plain flour
2 teaspoons baking powder
2 teaspoons ground ginger
2 teaspoons ground cinnamon
1 teaspoon ground cloves
½ teaspoon ground nutmeg
4 eggs
400 g granulated sugar
500 ml whipping cream
1 teaspoon vanilla essence
icing sugar, to decorate
pinch salt

Nutritional breakdown
(per portion)

Protein 9.0 g
Fat 10.1 g
Sugar 58.5 g
Carbohydrate 92.8 g
Energy 473 k cal

1 Preheat the oven to 180°C/Gas mark 4. Grease a 23-cm square baking tin.
2 Sift the **flour, baking powder, salt, ginger, cinnamon, cloves and nutmeg** into a bowl. Set aside.
3 With an electric mixer, beat the **eggs** on a high speed until very thick, for about 5 minutes. Gradually beat in the **granulated sugar**.
4 With the mixer on a low speed, beat the **flour and cream mixtures** into the **eggs**, alternating and beginning and ending with the **flour**. Stir in the **vanilla essence**.
5 Pour into the prepared tin and bake in the oven for 35 to 40 minutes, until the top of the cake springs back when touched lightly. Leave to cool in the tin on a wire rack for 10 minutes.

CHOCOLATE marshmallow brownies

Serves 12

75 g self-raising flour
4 tablespoons low-fat cocoa powder
½ teaspoon baking powder
¼ teaspoon salt
4 egg whites, whipped
75 g caster sugar
1 tablespoon vanilla essence
100 g marshmallows

Nutritional breakdown
(per portion)

Protein 2.2 g
Fat 0.1 g
Sugar 15.6 g
Carbohydrate 22.6 g
Energy 95 k cal

1 Preheat the oven to 190°C/Gas mark 5. Grease a non-stick 30 x 40-cm baking tin.

2 Sift the **flour, cocoa powder and baking powder** into a bowl, add the **salt** and mix together.

3 Beat the **egg whites** until stiff and then beat in the **sugar**. Add the **vanilla essence** and then mix in the **marshmallows**.

4 Pour the mixture into the prepared baking tin and bake in the oven for 15 to 17 minutes. It is cooked when no moisture attaches to a toothpick stuck into the mixture. Allow to cool slightly before dividing into brownie-sized pieces and removing from pan.

CHOCOLATE courgette brownies

Serves 8

4 courgettes, grated
1 banana, mashed
1 tablespoon water
2 teaspoons vanilla essence
300 g self-raising flour
1 ½ teaspoon baking powder
4 tablespoons low-fat cocoa powder
75 g caster sugar

Nutritional breakdown
(per portion)

Protein 4.5 g
Fat 0.7 g
Sugar 14.1 g
Carbohydrate 42.6 g
Energy 184 k cal

1 Preheat the oven to 200°C/Gas mark 7. Grease a non-stick 30 x 40-cm baking tin.

2 Mix together the **courgettes, banana, water and vanilla essence**.

3 In a separate bowl sift in the **flour, baking powder, cocoa powder and sugar**. Mix together and then add to the **wet ingredients**.

4 Pour into the prepared baking tin and bake in the oven for 25 to 30 minutes. The brownies are cooked when no moisture attaches to a toothpick stuck into the mixture. Allow to cool slightly before dividing into brownie-sized pieces and removing from pan.

Luscious advice

- **These brownies are great** served with fresh fruit or a sprinkle of icing sugar or low-fat ice cream.

- **Instead of courgettes,** try grated carrots, sultanas or a mix of sultanas and nuts. The courgettes and sultanas add fibre.

PIE crust one

1½ teaspoons low-fat margarine
150 g oatmeal
3 tablespoons brown sugar
1 egg white
6 tablespoons wheatgerm

Nutritional breakdown
(per portion)

Protein 3.5 g
Fat 2.4 g
Sugar 6.5 g
Carbohydrate 27.9 g
Energy 139 k cal

1 In a non-stick pan, melt the **margarine**. Add the **oatmeal** and toast until slightly golden.
2 Put the mixture into a bowl and add the **sugar, egg white and wheatgerm**. Mix.
3 Pat into pie dish and place in the refrigerator to cool for 30 minutes.

PIE crust two

1 tablespoon brown sugar
1 x 200 g low-fat digestive biscuits,
   crumbled and crushed to fine powder
2 tablespoon low-fat margarine
1 large egg white
1 teaspoon ground cinnamon

Nutritional breakdown
(per portion)

Protein 2.2 g
Fat 6.4 g
Sugar 5.3 g
Carbohydrate 19.1 g
Energy 137 k cal

1 Mix together the **sugar and biscuits**.
2 In a non-stick pan, melt the **margarine** and pour over the biscuit mix.
3 Whisk the **egg white** and mix in the bowl together with the **cinnamon**.
4 Pat into pie dish and place in the refrigerator to cool for 30 minutes.

PIE crust three

50 g low-fat butter or margarine
300 g self-raising flour
4 tablespoons custard powder
125 ml low-fat milk

Nutritional breakdown
(per portion)

Protein 4.2 g
Fat 3.3 g
Sugar 1.3 g
Carbohydrate 36.0 g
Energy 182 k cal

1 Mix together the **butter or margarine, flour and custard powder** and add the milk until a dough forms. Mix into a ball and chill in the refrigerator for 30 minutes.
2 Preheat the oven to 180°C/Gas mark 4.
3 Remove the dough from the refrigerator and roll out. Place over a greased pie dish and cut off the edges. Put some baking paper over the top and fill with dried rice or beans and bake in the oven for 10 minutes. Leave to cool.

LOW-FAT apple pie

Serves 8

150 g flour
75 g wheatgerm
2 tablespoons low-fat custard powder mix
1 egg
2 egg whites
125 ml skimmed milk
2 teaspoons baking soda
1 teaspoon baking powder
1 tablespoon ground cinnamon
1 tablespoon low-fat margarine
1 x 400 g can apple purée or 4 fresh apples
75 ml apple juice
75 ml honey, golden syrup or maple syrup
4 tablespoons sultanas
1 teaspoon cinnamon

Nutritional breakdown
(per portion)

Protein 9.0 g
Fat 2.7 g
Sugar 19.3 g
Carbohydrate 40.4 g
Energy 203 k cal

1 Preheat the oven to 180°C/Gas mark 4. Grease a non-stick pie dish.
2 Combine the **flour, wheatgerm, margarine, custard powder, egg, egg white, milk, baking soda and baking powder** and mix. Knead to form a dough. Roll out and spread over the pie dish. Keep the remaining mixture aside in the refrigerator, wrapped in plastic wrap. Bake for 10 minutes.
3 Meanwhile, in a non-stick pan, mix together the **apples, apple juice, honey, sultanas and cinnamon**. Stir until well cooked.
4 Take the pie from the oven and spoon in the mixture. Take the remaining **dough** from the refrigerator. Either cut into strips or cover the top of the pie completely. Put back into the oven until the top is golden brown (2–3 minutes).

LOW-FAT date and apple meringue pie

Serves 8

250 ml apple juice
2 teaspoons nutmeg or cinnamon
2 tablespoons caster sugar
2 x 400 g cans apple purée or 8 fresh apples
5 tablespoons sultanas
8 dates, chopped
4 egg whites
100 g caster sugar
pie crust of your choice (see page 134)

Nutritional breakdown
(per portion)

Protein 5.6 g
Fat 3.1 g
Sugar 52.3 g
Carbohydrate 73.7 g
Energy 321 k cal

1 Preheat the oven to 180°C/Gas mark 4.
2 In a non-stick pan combine the **juice with the spices and 2 tablespoons caster sugar** and stir for 3 minutes on medium heat. Add in the **fruit,** bring to the boil and boil for 2 minutes. Leave to cool.
3 In the meantime, beat together the **egg whites** and gradually add **100 g caster sugar**.
4 Take your pie crust and add the **fruit**. Top with the **whipped meringue**.
5 Place in the oven for 5 minutes constantly checking that the meringue hasn't burnt.

BREAD Pudding

Serves 8

75 g brown sugar
2 eggs
375 ml evaporated skimmed milk
2 teaspoons vanilla essence
1 teaspoon cinnamon
6 Granny Smith apples, peeled and chopped
5 slices just stale brown, white or fruit bread,
 cut into cubes

Nutritional breakdown
(per portion)

Protein 4.9 g
Fat 1.9 g
Sugar 20.7 g
Carbohydrate 28.5 g
Energy 141 k cal

1 Preheat the oven to 180°C/Gas mark 4.

2 Beat together the **brown sugar and eggs**. Add the **evaporated milk, vanilla and cinnamon** and keep beating. Throw the **apples and cubed bread** into the mixture and mix. Set aside for 5 minutes.

3 Then pour it into a greased baking dish, make sure you distribute the **bread and apples** evenly all over the pan.

4 Bake in the oven for 30 minutes. Check and bake for about another 15 minutes. It should come out golden brown. Sprinkle with some **icing sugar** and serve.

STRAWBERRY tarts

Serves 6

1 packet mini-meringue cases
250 ml low-fat strawberry yoghurt
2 teaspoons gelatine
125 ml warm water
8 strawberries, cut in half

Nutritional breakdown
(per portion)

Protein 6.6 g
Fat 2.7 g
Sugar 30.7 g
Carbohydrate 52.2 g
Energy 245 k cal

1 Mix the **gelatine and water** into the **yoghurt**.
2 Fill the mini-cases with the **yoghurt**.
3 Top with the **strawberries**.

PAVLOVA base

Serves 6

5 egg whites
1 teaspoon vinegar
1 teaspoon cornflour
175 g caster sugar
½ teaspoon vanilla essence

Nutritional breakdown
(per portion)

Protein 1.9 g
Fat 0.1 g
Sugar 23.2 g
Carbohydrate 23.8 g
Energy 97 k cal

1 Preheat the oven to 130°C/Gas mark ½.
2 Beat the **egg whites** with the **vinegar** and **half the cornflour** until very stiff. Beat in the **sugar and vanilla essence**.
3 Pile onto a greased and lined baking sheet, ensuring that there is a small well in the centre.
4 Bake in the oven for 1 ½ hours. Leave to cool before serving with the following topping.

PAVLOVA topping

Serves 6

250 ml low-fat strawberry yoghurt
   or crème fraiche
16 strawberries, chopped
75 g icing sugar

Nutritional breakdown
(per portion)

Protein 1.5 g
Fat 0.2 g
Sugar 16.7 g
Carbohydrate 16.8 g
Energy 71 k cal

1 Put the **yoghurt or crème fraiche** in the centre of the base.
2 Add the **strawberries**, top with the remaining **yoghurt** and sprinkle with **icing sugar**.

BLUEBERRY mousse

Makes 8 small ramekins

500 g canned or fresh blueberries
3 tablespoons caster sugar
2 tablespoons gelatine
250 ml skimmed evaporated milk
250 g low-fat yoghurt

Nutritional breakdown
(per portion)

Protein 6.5 g
Fat 0.4 g
Sugar 12.1 g
Carbohydrate 12.1 g
Energy 75 k cal

1 Purée the **blueberries** with the **sugar** – reserve the liquid, including any from the can. Warm the **blueberry liquid** and dissolve the **gelatine** in it.
2 Whip the **milk** until thick and beat in the **yoghurt**. Mix in the **gelatine** and fold in the **blueberry purée**. Place into individual bowls and chill.

CHOCOLATE and strawberry mousse

Makes 8 small ramekins

60 ml water
2 teaspoons gelatine powder
4 tablespoons low-fat cocoa powder
500 ml low-fat yoghurt
4 egg whites
½ teaspoon vanilla essence
75 g puréed strawberries
150 g caster sugar
1 tablespoon icing sugar
cocoa powder, to decorate

Nutritional breakdown
(per portion)

Protein 5.5 g
Fat 0.5 g
Sugar 27.1 g
Carbohydrate 27.2 g
Energy 129 k cal

1 Heat the water in a pan and add the **gelatine powder**. Remove from heat.
2 Mix the **cocoa powder** into the **yoghurt**.
3 Whip the **egg whites** until peaked, then add the **vanilla essence, strawberry purée and caster sugar**.
4 Mix the **ingredients** and spoon into small bowls. Refrigerate for 4 to 5 hours. Just before serving, decorate with **cocoa powder and icing sugar**.

GET CREAMY

Quark is a great low-fat replacement for cream and contains less than 1 per cent fat. It is a dairy product and is available in most supermarkets. As an alternative creamy addition to your food, use low-fat cream cheese or skimmed milk, as given in some of our recipes.

For each of these recipes, combine all the ingredients and serve as a cream. Depending on taste, you may need to add some extra sugar.

QUARK cream

Serves 4

250 ml quark
50 g caster sugar
1 teaspoon vanilla essence

Nutritional breakdown
(per portion)

Protein 9.1 g
Fat 0.1 g
Sugar 16.3 g
Carbohydrate 16.3 g
Energy 98 k cal

CHOCOLATE quark cream

Serves 4

250 ml quark
50 g caster sugar
1 teaspoon vanilla essence
1 tablespoon low-fat cocoa powder
  or 2 tablespoons chocolate syrup

Nutritional breakdown
(per portion)

Protein 9.3 g
Fat 0.1 g
Sugar 16.6 g
Carbohydrate 16.6 g
Energy 100 k cal

COFFEE quark cream

Serves 4

1 teaspoon instant coffee dissolved
  in 2 teaspoons of water
250 ml quark
50 g caster sugar
1 teaspoon vanilla essence

Nutritional breakdown
(per portion)

Protein 9.2 g
Fat 0.1 g
Sugar 6.3 g
Carbohydrate 16.4 g
Energy 99 k cal

VANILLA cream

Serves 4

100 g low-fat cream cheese
4 teaspoons icing sugar
2 teaspoons vanilla essence
4 tablespoons quark

Nutritional breakdown
(per portion)

Protein 5.5 g
Fat 0.4 g
Sugar 17.8 g
Carbohydrate 18.0 g
Energy 93 k cal

LOW-FAT cream topping

Serves 4

1 teaspoon gelatine
2 tablespoons water
200 ml evaporated skimmed milk, chilled
2 tablespoons sugar
1 teaspoon vanilla extract
2 teaspoons lemon juice

Nutritional breakdown
(per portion)

Protein 2.7 g
Fat 0.1 g
Sugar 11.1 g
Carbohydrate 11.1 g
Energy 53 k cal

1 Pour the **milk** into a bowl.
2 Sprinkle the **gelatine** over cold water in a small pan, then stir over a low heat until dissolved. Add to the **milk** and beat until stiff. Add the **sugar, vanilla and lemon juice**. Use immediately, or beat again before serving.

DELICIOUS DRINKS

Smoothies are fantastic as a liquid breakfast option or as a mini-meal. Non-dairy smoothies are particularly good as they are very low in fat. They can be served at any time.

You need to prepare by freezing the following fruit. To do this, just wash, top and tail berries and peel the fruit with skin. Chop and freeze in airtight bags. Here are some suggestions for fruit that freezes well:

- blueberries
- strawberries
- peaches
- mangoes
- raspberries.

For each of the recipes given below, each of which serves 2, simply prepare the fruit as described and blend and serve immediately. Bananas add creaminess. You can buy boxes of orange and apple juice, but freshly squeezed is best. However, it is good to have the boxes as a back-up.

Following on from the fruit smoothies below, we give you recipes for dairy smoothies. Change fat content by changing the milk type. They're great as a filler and also good with protein powder if you're working out at the gym.

STRAWBERRY smoothies

6 frozen strawberries, hulls removed
2 bananas, chopped
250 ml apple juice
125 ml orange juice

Nutritional breakdown
(per portion)

Protein 2.6 g
Fat 0.7 g
Sugar 45.2 g
Carbohydrate 47.0 g
Energy 194 k cal

MANGO mix

1 mango, chopped
2 bananas, chopped
250 ml apple juice
125 ml orange juice

Nutritional breakdown
(per portion)

Protein 2.6 g
Fat 0.7 g
Sugar 45.2 g
Carbohydrate 47.0 g
Energy 194 k cal

PEACHES in the park

3 peaches, chopped
2 bananas, chopped
250 ml orange juice
250 ml apple juice

Nutritional breakdown
(per portion)

Protein 2.6 g
Fat 0.7 g
Sugar 45.2 g
Carbohydrate 47.0 g
Energy 194 k cal

BERRIES are beaut

80 g mixed berries
2 bananas, chopped
250 ml orange juice
250 ml apple juice

Nutritional breakdown
(per portion)

Protein 2.6 g
Fat 0.7 g
Sugar 45.2 g
Carbohydrate 47.0 g
Energy 194 k cal

CHOC-o-holic

250 ml skimmed milk
2 tablespoons vanilla low-fat yoghurt
1 tablespoon low-fat chocolate powder
1 tablespoon low-fat ice cream
  or 2 tablespoons ice
1 banana, chopped (optional)

Nutritional breakdown
(per portion)

Protein 3.6 g
Fat 1.3 g
Sugar 34.3 g
Carbohydrate 36.3 g
Energy 163 k cal

ENERGY boost

250 ml skimmed milk
1 tablespoon honey
1 tablespoon low-fat vanilla yoghurt
1 tablespoon low-fat muesli or wheatgerm
1 tablespoon ice or low-fat ice cream
2 bananas, chopped

Nutritional breakdown
(per portion)

Protein 2.6 g
Fat 0.7 g
Sugar 45.2 g
Carbohydrate 47.0 g
Energy 194 k cal

ICE coffee

250 ml skimmed milk
5 ice cubes
1 tablespoon vanilla yoghurt
1 tablespoon low-fat ice cream

Nutritional breakdown
(per portion)

Protein 2.6 g
Fat 0.7 g
Sugar 45.2 g
Carbohydrate 47.0 g
Energy 194 k cal

CARAMEL cream

250 ml skimmed milk
1 tablespoon low-fat caramel topping
5 ice cubes
1 tablespoon vanilla low-fat yoghurt
2 tablespoons ice cream
1 banana, chopped

Nutritional breakdown
(per portion)

Protein 2.6 g
Fat 0.7 g
Sugar 45.2 g
Carbohydrate 47.0 g
Energy 194 k cal

STRAWBERRY milk shake

8 strawberries, hulled
300 ml skimmed milk
5 ice cubes
2 tablespoons yoghurt
1 banana, chopped

Nutritional breakdown
(per portion)

Protein 2.6 g
Fat 0.7 g
Sugar 45.2 g
Carbohydrate 47.0 g
Energy 194 k cal

Juicerator

In the new millennium, juices and juice mixes have been dubbed juice nutraceuticals. If you make your own, you guarantee your body a blast of nutrients – vital minerals and vitamins needed to boost your energy. The great thing about juice is that it is also a fabulous fat-free addition to a low-fat diet. If you mix and match fruits and vegetables you can get a sensational blast of flavours. Drinking fresh juice is also a great way to get your daily fruit and vegetable requirement.

Juices that are correctly juiced or blended can also be 'mini-meals'. Because they contain not just juice but also some fibre, they are great for curbing hunger pangs.

To juice properly you'll need a mini-juicing station. Here's what you will require:

> 1 Juicer or food processor.
> 2 Blender.
> 3 Orange juice squeezer .

There are various types of juicers and food processors available. Some food processors have attachments that allow you to squeeze citrus fruits; juice what we call a soft fruit like carrot, apple or celery; and also purée parsley and chilli. If you buy an all-in-one option you'll find you can also use it for other low-fat cooking such as cake-making. Ensure the one you choose meets the following requirements:

- It is easy to use.
- It is easy to clean – that means it doesn't have a million tiny pieces.
- It offers multiple uses.
- It has a choice of speeds.
- It is reasonably priced.
- If you need replacement parts, they are easy to find.
- It can fit in your kitchen.

For each of the recipes given overleaf, each of which serves 1, prepare the ingredients as appropriate, pop into your juicer, press the button and – hey presto! – you have a fantastic fortifying juice. Drink immediately.

APPLE angel

1 lemon, peeled
2-3 apples

Nutritional breakdown
(per portion)

Protein 3.6 g
Fat 1.3 g
Sugar 34.3 g
Carbohydrate 36.3 g
Energy 163 k cal

GINGER spice

knuckle-sized piece of ginger
1 orange, peeled
1 apple
2 carrots

Nutritional breakdown
(per portion)

Protein 3.6 g
Fat 1.3 g
Sugar 34.3 g
Carbohydrate 36.3 g
Energy 163 k cal

Luscious advice

• **You'll find** that over a period of time you'll find your tolerance to ginger increases and you'll want more in your juice.

• **Ginger spice is great** if you feel a cold coming on. It is rich in flu- fighting nutrients and the ginger clears the sinuses.

• **For extra kick** add some chilli juiced through your soft fruit juicer. It's a mind-blowing, cold-curing juice attack.

SUPER-C cold killer

1 lemon, peeled
1 lime, peeled
3 oranges, peeled

Nutritional breakdown
(per portion)

Protein 3.6 g
Fat 1.3 g
Sugar 34.3 g
Carbohydrate 36.3 g
Energy 163 k cal

VIRGIN Mary

2 sticks celery, chopped
handful of parsley
2 medium-sized carrots, chopped
4 tomatoes, chopped
1 teaspoon Worcestershire sauce
sprinkle freshly ground black pepper

Nutritional breakdown
(per portion)

Protein 3.6 g
Fat 1.3 g
Sugar 34.3 g
Carbohydrate 36.3 g
Energy 163 k cal

Luscious advice

• **Ensure your tomatoes** are fresh and preferably organic not greenhouse grown.

• **If you can't get** tomatoes keep a long-life pack of tomato juice in the cupboard. It is not as fresh but makes it easier to make your juice.

CELERY and apple juice

2 sticks celery, chopped
carrot and apple juice to top up

Nutritional breakdown
(per portion)

Protein 3.6 g
Fat 1.3 g
Sugar 34.3 g
Carbohydrate 36.3 g
Energy 163 k cal

SALSA crush

1 red, green or yellow pepper, deseeded
and chopped (if you want more kick,
leave the seeds in)
1 cm chilli
1 lemon, peeled
3 tomatoes, chopped

Nutritional breakdown
(per portion)

Protein 3.6 g
Fat 1.3 g
Sugar 34.3 g
Carbohydrate 36.3 g
Energy 163 k cal

Luscious advice

- **For extra spice** juice one stalk of spring onions.

- **You can heat** this juice up to become a soup.

- **This juice** is rich in Vitamin C and helps fight fatigue. Remember the
  more chilli you add, the more punch it has.

SALAD detox

2 stalks celery, chopped
handful of lettuce
3 florets broccoli
3 medium-sized carrots, chopped
2 tomatoes, chopped

Nutritional breakdown
(per portion)

Protein 3.6 g
Fat 1.3 g
Sugar 34.3 g
Carbohydrate 36.3 g
Energy 163 k cal

Luscious advice

- **You must stir** this juice well to combine the flavours.

- **Once stirred** pour this juice over ice cubes – ie helps spread the flavour.

- **Lettuce, broccoli** and celery have nutrients which help boost the immune system.

- **This juice** can also be heated to make a soup.

CUCUMBER and lettuce detox

2 stalks celery
handful lettuce leaves
handful frozen parsley
5 cm cucumber
carrot juice to top up

Nutritional breakdown
(per portion)

Protein 3.6 g
Fat 1.3 g
Sugar 34.3 g
Carbohydrate 36.3 g
Energy 163 k cal

Luscious advice

- **This juice** is a perfect detox option. It helps cleanse your system aided by cucumber, which is a natural diuretic.

- **This juice** also aids digestion.

- **If you'd like** to add more kick add chilli.

LUSCIOUS LISTS

The kitchen storecupboard

Here is the ultimate luscious storecupboard list. Follow this and you will always have just the ingredients in stock that you need to create most of the recipes in this book.

Spices and herbs

Spices are essential in low-fat cooking because they add flavour. You can start with the most basic of spices, but ensure that they are good quality. We recommend:

all spice

basil leaves, dried

black pepper corns and pepper grinder

chilli powder

cinnamon

cloves

coriander

cumin

curry powder

garlic

garlic powder

mint, dried

mustard powder

nutmeg

oregano

sage, dried

sea salt

sesame seeds

thyme leaves, dried

Remember that while fresh is always best it can be hard to find, so keep a well-stocked spice cupboard.

Fruit and vegetables

Try to ensure that you have a good selection of fruit and vegetables in stock at all times. These vegetables store especially well:

asparagus

baby spinach

carrots

celery

courgettes

lettuce, various varieties

mushrooms

peas

potatoes

red onions (better colour and flavour than Spanish)

sweetcorn

tomatoes

Canned products

With a few fresh ingredients and a few canned ingredients we'll show how you can create gourmet low fat meals easily. Here is what we recommend for your canned product stockpile:

baked beans, low-fat

coconut milk, low-fat

evaporated milk, skimmed

fruit:
  apricots, in own juice
  peaches, in own juice
  pineapple, in own juice
fish:
  salmon, in brine
  tuna, in brine
salsa
sweetcorn
taco sauce
tomato purée
tomatoes, peeled and chopped

PACKED PRODUCTS
crackers, low-fat
crisps, low-fat
couscous
custard, low-fat
dried beans, selection of
dried fruit:
  apples
  apricots
  dates
  fruit salad
  raisins
  sultanas
juices:
  cranberry
  tomato
milk:
  condensed, skimmed
  skimmed
  soya
olives, in brine
pasta, selection of

porridge oats
rice, brown, wild
snack bars, low-fat
taco crisps, baked
Bottles with flavour
balsamic vinegar
chilli sauce
jams, reduced sugar
olive oil, good quality
mayonnaise, low-fat
mustard
sesame oil
soy sauce, good quality
oyster sauce
taco sauce
vanilla essence

ITEMS FOR THE FRIDGE
cheese, low-fat
eggs
fruit juices, freshly squeezed
milk, low-fat
yoghurt, low-fat

ITEMS FOR THE FREEZER
beans
bread, brown
fruit (buy peaches, strawberries and other exotics in season, wash them and freeze)
ice cream, low-fat
mixed vegetable
peas
pitta bread
sweetcorn
yoghurt, low-fat

The fat-finding chart

Here is a chart that outlines the average fat contents of the most frequently eaten foods. See also page 8 to further your knowledge about fat and what and what not to eat. This chart is intended as a guide only. Consult your doctor or a dietitian for more information. Some products may vary in fat content due to different production techniques.

Dairy products	Fat (g)
butter (1 teaspoon)	4.00
cheese:	
blue vein (30 g)	10.00
Brie (30 g)	8.70
Cheddar (30 g)	10.00
cottage (100 g)	3.90
cream cheese with fruit (30 g)	6.90
Edam (30 g)	8.00
Feta (30 g)	7.50
Feta, reduced fat (30 g)	4.40
Parmesan, grated (10 g)	3.20
Cream cheese, full fat (100 g)	30.00
Cream cheese, low-fat (100 g)	15.00
processed cheese slices (100 g)	27.00
processed cheese slices, light (100 g)	10.00
ricotta, regular (100 g)	11.00
ricotta, reduced fat (100 g)	8.30
ricotta, low-fat (10 g)	4.60
margarine (1 tsp)	4.00
milk:	
full cream (250 ml)	9.80
semi-skimmed (250 ml)	4.00
skimmed (250 ml)	0.25

Bread

bread:	
brown, thin (1 slice)	0.90
brown, thick (1 slice)	1.20
white, thin (1 slice)	0.70
white, thick (1 slice)	0.90
toast (thin slice + 1 tsp butter)	4.70
toast (thick slice + 2 tsps butter)	8.90
croissant (medium)	11.50
croissant (large)	16.50
crumpet (without topping)	0.50
French toast (1 slice)	6.50
naan bread (50 g)	5.80
rye, dark (1 slice)	0.50
rye, light (1 slice)	0.60

Cereal

bran (half cup)	1.40
crunchy nut flakes (1 cup)	1.20
muesli, toasted (60 g)	10.70
muesli, natural (60 g)	4.40
oat bran flakes (one cup)	1.70
porridge (1 cup)	2.50
porridge cooked in milk/water	5.50

Snacks and nuts

chips, fried (25 g)	11.40
brazil nuts (100 g)	68.00
cashews, roasted (100 g)	51.00
corn chips, plain (50 g)	9.60
corn chips, cheesy (50 g)	11.00
crisps (50 g packet)	16.80
crisps, low-fat (see page 00)	3.40
peanuts, plain (100 g)	46.00

peanuts, roasted (100 g)	53.00
pine nuts (100 g)	68.60
popcorn, plain (1 cup)	2.00
popcorn, no oil (1 cup)	0.30
popcorn (cinema serve)	6.50
pretzels (50 g)	3.50

Dips (4 tablespoons)

caviar	29.60
eggplant	11.60
hummus	10.00
guacamole	25.20
jalapeno bean	2.80
salsa, low-fat (see page 00)	0.40
taramosalata	29.60
tzatziki	6.40

Meat

beef:

corned beef, fatty (2 slices)	12.90
corned beef, lean (2 slices)	3.50
mince, fatty (100 g)	16.10
mince, lean (100 g)	6.70
steak, medium steak (150 g)	15.00
steak medium lean (150 g)	7.00

chicken:

raw breast fillet, skinless	2.30
raw breast fillet, with skin	10.20
quarter, roasted skinless	7.70
quarter, roasted, with skin	20.00
wing, roasted, skinless	5.00
wing, fried, with skin	10.00

lamb:

loin chop, with fat	22.00
loin chop, lean	1.80

pork:

ham off bone (30 g)	2.30
prosciutto, thin slice	8.00

sausage, thin (grilled)	9.80
sausage, thick (grilled)	15.20

turkey:

roasted, skinless (100 g)	1.50
roasted, with skin (100 g)	6.50
roll	1.30

Fish

salmon:

pink (100g can)	6.00
raw fillet	19.50

tuna:

in brine (100 g can)	2.00
in oil (100 g can)	11.00
raw fillet (150 g)	0.80

Meals

beef vindaloo (250 g)	16.00
bolognese sauce (300 g) 14	
carbonara (300 g)	31.00
chicken pilau (200 g)	23.00
curry puff, meat (30 g)	11.00
garlic prawns (three)	16.00
lamb kebab, skewer	6.00
lasagne, meat (400 g)	24.00
pasta, plain (1 cup)	0.80
pesto sauce (300 g)	22.00
poppadums, each	2.50
samosas, each	11.00
spring rolls, small, each	5.00
Thai chicken curry	42.00
vegetable stir-fry	10.00

Fast food

fish (battered, deep fried)	23.00
fish and chips	48.00
doner kebab in Lebanese bread	20.00
falafel (per 30-g piece)	4.00

guacamole + corn chips	35.00
nachos (single serve)	21.00
pastie/meat pie	26.00

Biscuits (each)

choc chip cookies	2.40
digestive, plain	2.70
digestive, chocolate	4.30
gingernut	1.20
shortbread	4.80
water cracker	0.60

Cakes (per serving)

apple strudel	20.00
black forest gateau	19.00
banana cake	15.00
carrot cake	30.00
carrot cake, low-fat	8.00

cheesecake 130g	29.00
choc brownie	20.00
choc brownie, low-fat	8.00
Danish pastry	17.60
doughnut (plain)	10.30
muffins, full fat	20.00
pecan pie	26.00

Desserts

apple pie	15.00
banana split	32.00
bread and butter pudding	18.00
chocolate mousse (80 g)	18.00
creme brulée	30.00
creme caramel	26.20
ice cream:	
1 scoop	12.00
deluxe	18.00

Useful addresses

LUSCIOUS HEAD OFFICE

159 Praed St
London W2IRL
www.luscious.co.uk

For the address of our low fat cafés in London email: Info@luscious.co.uk
If you ever have any problems and need help finding products we'll do what we can.

Alison@luscious.co.uk
Tony@luscious.co.uk

Luscious likes to use organic food whenever possible. For the addresses of Luscious organic corner stores visit our website or telephone: 020 7262 9492.

Or sauces, marinades and organic products can be ordered from:
Planet Organic
42 Westbourne Grove
London W25SH

Mail order organic products

You can mail organic food online at: www.simplyorganic.net

www.tesco.com or other supermarket online shopping services can also help you search for products that may be hard to find.

Exercise is also vital, so check out:
www.exercise.com
www.healthyeating.com
www.healthy.net

Index

luscious lists

Author's acknowledgments

Thank you to Jacquie Burns for her faith in the book, Emma Callery for her patience editing and Catherine Lappin, Tracey Batenburg, the Luscious Chefs, managers and staff for helping write and produce this book. It couldn't have been done without you.

Vermilion books may be obtained from any good bookshop or by telephoning TBS Direct on: 01206 255 800